brilliant

persuasion

brilliant

persuasion

Everyday techniques to boost your powers of persuasion

Stephen C. Young

Harlow, England • London • New York • Boston • San Francisco • Toronto • Sydney • Auckland • Singapore • Hong Kong
Tokyo • Seoul • Taipei • New Delhi • Cape Town • São Paulo • Mexico City • Madrid • Amsterdam • Munich • Paris • Milan

PEARSON EDUCATION LIMITED

Edinburgh Gate
Harlow CM20 2JE
United Kingdom
Tel: +44 (0)1279 623623
Web: www.pearson.com/uk

First edition published 2017 (print and electronic)

ISBN: 978-1-292-13573-1 (print)
      978-1-292-13574-8 (PDF)
      978-1-292-13575-5 (ePub)

British Library Cataloguing-in-Publication Data
A catalogue record for the print edition is available from the British Library

Library of Congress Cataloging-in-Publication Data
A catalog record for the print edition is available from the Library of Congress

10 9 8 7 6 5 4 3 2 1
20 19 18 17 16

Print edition typeset in Plantin MT Pro 10/14 pts by SPi Global
Printed in Malaysia (CTP-PJB)

NOTE THAT ANY PAGE CROSS REFERENCES REFER TO THE PRINT EDITION

Contents

Acknowledgements

I thank my editor, Eloise Cook, for having the confidence in me to write this important addition to the Brilliant series. And to Sarah Owens, the copy-editor, and Melanie Carter and Dhanya Ramesh who have painstakingly guided me through the process of producing this book.

I'd also like to warmly thank my dear friends Jinnie and Denis Moriarty for their infinite patience, continual moral support and words of encouragement from concept to completion of this first edition of *Brilliant Persuasion*.

Publisher's acknowledgements

We are grateful to the following for permission to reproduce copyright material:

Photo on p. 165 © Tom Merton/Getty Images; photo on p. 166 © ASDF_MEDIA/Shutterstock; photo on p. 167 © Marcos Mesa/Sam Wordley/Shutterstock; photo on p. 168 © wavebreak-media/Shutterstock; photo on p. 169 © Hinterhaus Productions/ Getty Images; photo on p. 170 © PhotoAlto/Eric Audras/Getty Images; photo on p. 173 © Compassionate Eye Foundation/ David Oxberry/Getty Images; photo on p. 174 © PhotoAlto/Eric Audras/Getty Images.

About the author

Stephen C. Young is, foremost, an entrepreneur and, today, a leading trainer and founder of Proactive Persuasion, a UK consultancy delivering unique immersion-style training seminars about persuasion.

He grew up and was educated in Newcastle upon Tyne. After leaving school, he spent a short time as an electrical engineer. His sales career started in 1978 when he joined the city's principle daily newspaper, *The Evening Chronicle*. For two years, he worked in the challenging world of advertising sales before, in 1980, relocating to London to take up an appointment at the Foreign & Commonwealth Office (FCO).

Experiencing first-hand the high cost of living in the Capital, and with three weeks to wait before taking up his new post, he investigated more lucrative, alternative opportunities. Within a week, he was offered and accepted a business development role selling high-value recruitment services at more than triple the salary offered by the FCO.

In 1993, he established Stephen St James & Associates, an executive search and selection consultancy, specialising in information technology and telecommunications recruitment, located in Central London's prestigious Bedford Square. He managed and grew this business, employing and training a team of specialists over the next 13 years.

In 2010, having reviewed numerous technical volumes on the subject of persuasion and influence, he discovered that, throughout most of his career, he naturally, without conscious awareness, applied in everyday conversations linguistic techniques known as language patterns. He believes passionately that everyone can be more persuasive in their daily lives once they also become aware of the particular nuances of persuasive linguistics.

In the same way that everyone can play random notes on a piano and only some can play a tune, everyone can talk, but only those skilled in the art of persuasion understand the importance of arranging words in the right order! A compilation of simple linguistic techniques used by the most capable sales professionals in the world, *Brilliant Persuasion* will reveal that order.

Stephen lives in West London and, some would say, is a coffee, red wine and gym addict. He divides his time between the United Kingdom and Latin America with occasional visits catching up with friends and family in Newcastle upon Tyne.

Foreword

Here is a book you might want to take a look at with excitement.

What is important to you about being more persuasive? Success, status, recognition or something else? This book will challenge, delight and inform you. It will also change you.

I have known Stephen Young for over 25 years. Our paths first crossed when we worked together at Europe's first executive search firm specialising in the technology industry. I quickly formed a strong respect and liking for an individual with a solid work ethic married to a very positive and outgoing personality.

Our paths have taken on a comparable quality. We both went on to run our successful executive search businesses, and today we share a profound interest in human motivation and persuasion. We have both had our demons and exorcised them. I was, therefore, both pleased and flattered when he asked me to write the Foreword to this book.

A few years ago, we met again to discuss a new project: a consultancy service delivering immersion-style seminars about persuasion and influence to all industry sectors. At that stage, it was only an embryo in Stephen's mind. His passion for what was to become Proactive Persuasion (www.proactivepersuasion.com) made a vivid impression on me and I was keen to learn more. Over the next few years and many meetings, the project took on a definite shape and a sharp focus. I listened avidly and devoured the material.

Since then, I have used a raft of persuasion techniques, revealed in *Brilliant Persuasion,* in my career management practice to significant effect. Moreover, I have transmitted them, in turn, to my clients, who have implemented them with very positive results.

I, like many others, have come to realise that proactive persuasion is a powerful stealth weapon in the interpersonal communications arsenal. There is no doubt in my mind that, as such, it should be right at the top of everyone's essential business and personal development skills shopping list.

The benefits of this book and the training that underpins it are self-evident. I have, personally, witnessed that training and have watched fascinated as I saw the light of revelation dawn on the faces of the course participants. From that point onwards, their interactions with others were of a different, more dynamic nature. In at least one case it led, within just 24 hours, to an individual closing three major new business contracts with a hitherto intransigent client. Seeing is believing.

In writing *Brilliant Persuasion,* Stephen has achieved something else quite remarkable. As a resourcing and careers professional, I have waded through many scholarly tomes, quite a few of which on the awe-inspiring subject of neuro-linguistic programming, or NLP. These books should come with painkillers. They are, usually, highly academic, often abstruse and invariably turgid. Based on NLP, but wondrously without the tiresome and often impenetrable jargon, *Brilliant Persuasion* provides powerfully practical linguistic tools for ordinary people.

It distils the psychology of persuasion into simple step-by-step techniques that anyone can learn. However, you will not just learn; you will understand and, crucially, act. That is hugely valuable in today's world, where we are all saturated with information and are time-poor.

Sometimes, we are, indeed, so busy with our lives we forget who we are and, much more importantly, whom we wish to become. However, through diligent study, reflection and application, we can progress as individuals and, if we are persistent, transformation occurs, and this can operate on many levels.

This book will get you there.

James Ashmore, LifeWork, Kent,
United Kingdom, March 2015

Introduction

Language patterns – persuasion or manipulation?

The most important persuasion tool you have in your entire arsenal is integrity.

Zig Ziglar (1926–2012) author, salesman and
motivational speaker

You may have come across *Brilliant Persuasion* as an electronic download or, maybe, you are in a bookshop right now reading every word. Perhaps you know someone who has attended a Proactive Persuasion Seminar and they have lent you what they, undoubtedly, consider to be the *Bible of Persuasion.* However you have discovered *Brilliant Persuasion,* it will positively change the way you think about using language to persuade.

In every aspect of our day-to-day lives, it is essential to be able to influence others, isn't it? Particularly at work, with ever increasing pressure always to over-achieve and to be someone your contemporaries and superiors will revere and the competition will fear. If you are a self-employed entrepreneur, having the skills to convince and engender interest and curiosity consistently in your products and services can mean the difference between foreclosure and bankruptcy or a level of wealth only you can imagine.

If you are employed full-time or retained on a freelance basis, managing your own business or currently exploring recruitment opportunities, imagine what it would be like to feel intensely secure about your future as you consistently exceed your targets and secure the most profitable contracts. Doubtless, you are already beginning to realise you hold in your hands the means of achieving your goal.

Brilliant Persuasion is a practical step-by-step guide developed to ensure your future security by intensifying your powers of persuasion and influence far beyond their current levels. You will discover real-world techniques that you will apply to everyday situations where you need to change somebody's mind or influence and encourage them to accede willingly to your point of view.

Curiously, it is possible that you already use some of the persuasive language revealed in this book without being aware. However, it is more than likely you have little idea of the hidden power of your vocabulary. The more you read every word, the more you will notice how stress-free it is going to be to become more persuasive, and we are enthused to have the opportunity to guide you step by step through the process and reveal how you will be able to accomplish this more quickly than you believed possible.

Other publications about persuasion often shroud the subject in mystery and, worse still, make it appear more complicated than necessary. That is why in *Brilliant Persuasion* we have removed the jargon. The issue is not about the technical names of the techniques we reveal. The issue is how quickly you assimilate the techniques into your daily conversations and enjoy tangible, quantifiable results from doing so. That means having fun in the knowledge that you are following in the footsteps of some of the most successful sales and business development professionals in the world.

With *Brilliant Persuasion* you will learn quickly and use frequently covert conversational techniques known as language patterns. Moreover, as you think about acquiring these impressive skills, you will realise how using them will change your life.

Imagine the increased rewards and benefits you will enjoy when you start to use the techniques revealed in this book. We like this, because if you are currently in a sales role, you will begin to notice how smoothly and quickly, with just a little practice, you will be able to overcome all objections. Imagine! What would being able to do this mean to you? Think about it.

If you are a manager, persuading your team to follow a challenging path, you will enjoy learning how to bring everyone swiftly on board.

If you are seeking promotion or attending job interviews, the new skills you will have gained once you have read every word in this book will enable you to enjoy significant advantages over others unaware of these techniques. Now think about it, a person can get really motivated about this, can't you?

It is fair to say that the techniques you will learn in *Brilliant Persuasion* will enable you to build deeper levels of rapport, lower resistance and increase responsiveness to you and the messages you are delivering. As you read this now and absorb the significance, yet simplicity, of the techniques, you will appreciate how useful and powerful they are. Most importantly, though, you will begin to understand exactly how you will start to use them every day.

Warning

Because language patterns are so powerful, we have to guide you forward towards the most efficient way to deploy them; having said that, we cannot, of course, control how you, ultimately, decide to use your new-found skills.

We urge you always to use the information in this book carefully and only in situations of mutual gain. By doing so, your reputation will strengthen and grow, more people will want to work with you and it is very likely that you will be on your client's personal speed dial list. Imagine becoming the 'go to' person for everyone.

Using language patterns like this means you are using them to persuade.

Now, if you want to use language patterns without mutual gain, what began as a genuine ethical desire to persuade becomes manipulation. Your potential commercial partner may feel uncomfortable, you may still be awarded the job, sell the product/service or gain agreement, but, it will never be repeated. Your reputation will be tarnished forever and it is possible that you will become someone with whom others will prefer never to engage.

Proceed with care and enjoy the journey.

Brilliant Persuasion is divided into four parts:

Part 1: Talking to the subconscious – embedding commands and suggestions

The first part of this book looks at the subconscious. Initially, the clinical psychologists who used this technique reckoned it was too dangerous for release to the general public. Training was restricted and very expensive. Today, this inspirational, yet formidable, style of communication permeates the airways. Most multinationals, government officials and those business development professionals aware of this technique routinely use it every day to persuade and influence others. If you are not using it, be prepared because your competition unquestionably is!

Part 2: Persuasive language patterns

The second part of the book is devoted to a selection of the most persuasive techniques available, modelled after the communication style of some of the most persuasive and successful sales professionals in the world. The techniques you are about to discover will enable you to:

● Instantly resolve objections and lead sales conversation towards your goal – *The redefine.*

- Effortlessly remove resistance and increase rapport – *The agreement frame.*

- Subconsciously add and delete thoughts and reverse objections – *Linguistic mathematics.*

- Instantly establish resonant rapport – *Rapport.*

- Intensify your powers of influence – *Because logic.*

- Gain, unconditionally, acceptance of everything you say – *Awareness patterns.*

- Rapidly gain agreement and bypass criticism – *Verbal pacing and leading.*

- Magically resolve every objection with empathy and understanding – *Feel felt found.*

- Secretly direct others to think what you want them to think – *Internal representations.*

- Discover the hidden driving force compelling your prospect to make purchasing decisions – *Motivational direction.*

- Decipher the secret messages revealed in your prospects' eyes – *eye accessing cues.*

- Weakening objections and embedding suggestions – *Parts theory.*

- Plant suggestions without saying a word – *The quotes pattern.*

- Command attention with non-verbal communication – *Persuasive body language.*

Part 3: Persuasive questioning technique

In the third part you will discover how some questions are more powerful than others. Equipped with this insightful information, you will quantum leap your persuasive abilities and questioning technique, making it possible to take greater control of any conversation and be able to lead and direct your prospects and colleagues towards your goals. Asking the right questions is at the heart of effective communication and information exchange.

However, not only will you elicit information with carefully constructed questions, you will plant positive suggestions into the minds of your prospects even without their awareness; you will gain instant agreement and even enable your prospects to experience the most persuasive powerful experience of all, their imagination! We'll show you how to:

- Make it easy for your prospects by generously providing them with the answers you want – *with pre-suppositional questions.*

- Gain spontaneous agreement – *with tag questions.*

- Open your prospects' minds, stimulate curiosity and covertly plant suggestions – *with powerful questions.*

- Make your prospects crave your products – *with future pacing or time-travel questions.*

- Link what your prospects want to the benefits of your product – *with criteria questions.*

Part 4: Preparing to persuade

In the final part the tables are turned as we present a set of tantalising questions designed to force you to think outside of the box and to enhance your focus and overall preparedness. We'll show you a proven technique to boost your confidence level far beyond what you ever thought achievable, and to improve your proficiency we'll show how to practice using language patterns.

- Prepare yourself for every outcome and consequence – *Questions to ask yourself* (Cartesian and pre-contact questions).

- Develop the confidence to persuade – *Building natural confidence.*

- Practise makes sales – *How to practise.*

PART 1

Talking to the subconscious

CHAPTER 1

Embedded commands and suggestions

Talking to the subconscious

'The conscious mind may be compared to a fountain playing in the sun and falling back into the great subterranean pool of subconscious from which it rises.'

Sigmund Freud

What are embedded commands?

I am delighted to present one of the most powerful persuasion techniques in existence. However, before we reveal how embedded commands are used, let's first determine what they are.

Embedded commands are suggestions made up of single words, such as: go, buy, like, stop; and short phrases when said in a particular fashion that communicate messages directly to the subconscious minds of others.

Why we use embedded commands

The reason we introduce embedded commands into sales conversation is to place ideas about our product or service or suggest actions we want our prospect to undertake or think about, in a way that bypasses their conscious awareness. In other words, we make a direct connection to their subconscious mind. Our aim is to communicate subliminal suggestions that create mental activity without conscious awareness.

I can almost read the thoughts of many of you as you digest these words. Please relax, this is not as sinister as you may, initially, suppose. Most of us are unaware that we do this all the time because it is normal conversation. It becomes a formidable persuasive technique only when we choose to use it.

Why embedding commands will work for you

Everything we hear, read and see can be appraised, condemned, argued and talked about or thrown away and rejected. However, concepts, ideas and suggestions conveyed subliminally to the unconscious mind encounter no opposition. This information is stored in the brain and affects the way we think, the decisions we make and the actions we take.

I remember an occasion when introducing embedded commands at a Proactive Persuasion Seminar. One delegate, concerned about appearing foolish, resolved to talk with others, rather than undertake the next practical exercise. I listened to their conversation, which went something like this:

Delegate one   Each time I try something like this, I always make a mistake.

Delegate two   But, you'll learn to embed commands faster than you thought possible, because you are doing it already.

Unknowingly, delegate one was more of an expert than they believed, as their statement contained at least two embedded messages that bypass the conscious mind. Delegate two, having a little more experience, purposefully chose to coach delegate one. We will analyse their dialogue later, and you will understand how it clearly demonstrates how most people integrate subliminal suggestions unknowingly into their everyday speech.

In this chapter, you will learn how to formulate suggestions and commands appropriate to your business, and you will discover how to articulate them correctly for maximum effectiveness. As you progress, you will begin to appreciate the importance of speaking clearly and how not doing so often creates the opposite outcome to that which you may have desired initially.

Because the medical professions noticed how everyone naturally *passively* embedded commands in everyday conversation, they realised the immense benefits that could be achieved by *actively* using these technique with patients, to guide and lead their thoughts and change their beliefs. It was not long before the sales/ marketing community latched onto this powerful linguistic technique.

Consider this: if you tell, order, instruct or command someone to do something or think about something in a particular way, almost invariably they will object, finding reasons why not to carry out your request. Sometimes, people will choose to do the exact opposite. I imagine you are familiar with this scenario, particularly if you have had children, as it seems to be human nature.

In our daily business encounters, it would be brilliant if we could merely tell our customers and prospects to sign up or buy our products and services, appoint us or even like us and expect them to do as we request, wouldn't it? *Actively* embedding commands into ordinary conversation will enable you to do just this. Now, a person can get enthused about being able to do this, can't you?

The concept of embedding commands into everyday conversations and bypassing the conscious minds of others is not without its sceptics, who question if it is possible to influence the minds of others, like this. In point of fact, as we've already mentioned most people are mindfully unaware that they are already experts at doing it!

If we return to the conversation I overheard while delivering a Proactive Persuasion Seminar, notice that I have highlighted the embedded commands used by both delegates:

Delegate one	Each time I try something *like this*, I always *make a mistake*.
Delegate two	But, you'll *learn to embed commands* faster than you thought possible, because you are doing it already.
Analysis	Delegate one embedded the commands *like this* and *make a mistake*. Neither makes sense

contextually. Delegate two, being more aware, suggested he/she would *learn to embed commands,* instructing delegate two to do just that! The conscious brain accepts the meaning of the whole statement. The subconscious, on the other hand, detects only the positive intent of the command.

This example demonstrates conclusively how most people unknowingly mix commands and suggestions into everyday conversations, unaware of the unconscious impact some of their words may have on others and, for that matter, themselves, particularly if they continually reinforce negative statements.

Visualise the increased rewards you will acquire by proactively using this technique. You will enjoy consistently quantifiable improved results, increased personal financial status; you will be able to engender successfully greater levels of rapport and influence, benefit from escalating levels of repeat business, and all the other advantages only you can imagine.

Of course, now, we are not alone in the use of embedded commands, times have changed considerably since their first discovery, they are ubiquitous. Large corporates pay millions to advertising agencies to lead and direct the purchasing decisions of an unsuspecting general public. Surprisingly, though, they do not always get it right. Recently, I heard a television commercial for a well-known brand of soft cheese, possibly named after the fifth-most-populous city in the United States. Below, we present the last few words of the advertisement, which is, presumably, the crucial message the advertiser wanted to leave in the minds of the viewers and potential customers:

It's so creamy it's too good to resist.

Have you already identified the glaring error? This particular promotion might have been more effective, and cost efficient, if the final wording had reinforced a positive action that the advertiser desired the viewers/listeners to perform, rather than emphasising something they would find, 'good to resist!' The closing image of the advertisement was of an actor consuming the product while, simultaneously, my subconscious mind, the moment it heard 'good to resist', was, without my awareness, considering the many ways I could, in fact, resist the item.

You, like me, will start hearing these glaring errors frequently. It is on occasions such as this that I often think how wonderful it would be to approach the managing directors of these global corporations privately, and point out the fundamental mistakes made by their highly prized and costly city advertising agents. The message we wish to impart in this story is to ensure you do not make the same blunders when promoting your products or services.

brilliant tip

Always precisely state what you mean in an unambiguous manner and consider how others might interpret your words, subconsciously. Moreover, learn to use this unique insight to *your* advantage at all times.

Once you start to see embedded commands, you will notice how often they are used in this chapter, on television, radio commercials and the sides of buses. In fact, everywhere. You will realise how politicians lead their unsuspecting interviewers to ask only the questions they wish to answer and, crucially, you will be more aware when others use them on you!

Having just mentioned politicians, I would like to introduce you to a section of Tony Blair's July 2003 speech to the US Congress. Here it is:

Thank you, Mr Speaker and Mr Vice-President, honourable members of Congress. I'm deeply touched by that warm and generous welcome. That's more than I deserve and more than I'm used to, quite frankly.

And let me begin by thanking you most sincerely for voting to award me the Congressional Gold Medal. But you, like me, know who the real heroes are: those brave service men and women, yours and ours, who fought the war and risk their lives still. And our tribute to them should be measured in this way, by showing them and their families that they did not strive or die in vain, but that, through their sacrifice, future generations can live in greater peace, prosperity and hope.

Were you able to spot the subliminal message? Read it again if you did not. In this speech, Blair is giving the listeners an explicit instruction to do something, and it is not intended to be consciously noticed by anyone, he is commanding the audience to like him.

Here it is:

And let me begin by thanking you most sincerely for voting to award me the Congressional Gold Medal. But you, like me, *know who the real heroes are.*

In this example, the command 'you like me' was embedded into the speech and, because of the way Blair delivers the words, they are interpreted literally by the subconscious minds of the listeners. Their conscious minds do not realise the underlying meaning, hearing only the overarching message. Was this done deliberately? Who knows? However, it is a technique you can start to adopt, isn't it?

---

brilliant action

Did you notice and appreciate the meaning of the 'You like me', 'I like you' language pattern when you first read it? Tony Blair's speech was not the first time it appeared. If you missed it, re-read this chapter to this point.

Creating and delivering embedded commands and suggestions

It is incredibly easy to devise and deliver embedded commands. Often, describing the method appears far more complicated than the techniques themselves. There are only two steps to follow, and each has its set of simple guidelines on which we will elaborate later. First, decide what you wish your prospect to do, to think about or act upon and, then second, carefully introduce these suggestions into the conversation in a manner that bypasses conscious awareness, similar to the technique we mentioned earlier, used by Tony Blair.

Creating embedded commands

When talking with their prospects and clients, most sales, marketing and business development professionals employ similar commands and, as you become more confident with their use, you will, spontaneously, create suggestions not only contextually appropriate with your working environment, but also, and most importantly, in keeping with your personal style of communication. To maximise their effectiveness, it is essential to keep commands brief, up to four words, and to use everyday language. The phrases below are short commands that you have, almost certainly, used without realising. It is also equally likely you did not deliver them in the most efficient manner. We will illustrate how to articulate commands a little later.

Examples of commands:

By now (buy)	By this (buy)
Like me/this	Try this
Trust me	Start today/now
Decide now/today	Believe me
Want this	Need to start now
Need to own	I need this
I can afford this	I want this
Work with Co. Name	Feel confident
Feel comfortable	Feel good
Be positive	Be happy
Ready to buy now	Fix another meeting
Be enthused	Be excited
Looks good	Register now
Making the right decision	Do what I say
Agree with me	Sign up today
Give us the go ahead	

From this list you can deduce that embedded commands are verbs implying an action, thought or emotion that we want others to do, to think about or feel. We have purposefully avoided the infinitive, the 'ing' form of the verb, because configurated like this it can act as an adjective and has the effect of weakening command statements.

Research indicates that our brains are hard-wired to create mental images of the verbs we hear. We call these mental images internal representations. It is also accepted that there are distinct regions of the brain that react faster to verbs than to nouns. Moreover, subconsciously, the brain is continuously on the lookout for linguistic patterns, rhythmic speech and powerful verbs.

brilliant tip

Review the list of verbs below and incorporate the most relevant ones into your presentations, sales letters, brochures, emails and texts.

Power verbs – action commands:

A abolish, achieve, act, adopt, align, anticipate, apply, assess, avoid, add.

B boost, buy, break, bridge, build, burn, bring.

C carry out, capture, can, change, choose, clarify, confront, confirm, connect, conquer, convert, create.

D define, decide, deploy, deliver, defuse, design, develop, diagnose, drive, divide.

E ensure, establish, evaluate, exploit, explore.

F filter, finalise, find, finance, focus, fix, follow.

G gain, gather, go, get, grasp.

I identify ignite, illuminate, improve, increase, innovate, invent, inspire, intensify, increase, initiate, invest.

K know, keep.

L lead, learn, leverage, light up.

M manage, master, maximise, measure, meet, mobilise, motivate, make.

O overpower, oppose.

P persuade, plan, position, prepare, prevent, produce, profit, purchase, proceed.

R raise, realise, reconsider, review, reduce, relish, refresh, replace, resist, retain, remove.

S save, scan, see, send, simplify, shorten, solve, stretch, succeed, supplement, start, speed up, show, spot.

T take, train, transfer, try, think again, trust.

U understand, unleash, use.

W want, whittle down, win.

Complexity of language

The commands that produce the best results are short-use everyday language and are often repeated. To enable us to restate suggestions undetected we use different words to say the same thing always beginning with the simplest vocabulary. For example, we might say:

- Buy or get, then purchase or acquire or procure
- Start or begin, then initiate or commence
- Go then proceed
- Send or post, then dispatch or deliver
- Find or spot, then locate or identify or source
- See then observe and so on.

Think about the mental pictures the brain must construct to understand these words. The more complex the language, the more ineffective the command. For example, it is far easier for the brain to extract meaning by making internal representations for the statement, '*buy* this *now*', rather than *procure* this *straightaway*.

Buy and now are easier concepts to understand than procure and straightaway.

Introducing embedded commands into conversation with weasel or opening phrases

You will find, when you use embedded commands, that they are more powerful, practically unnoticeable and readily accepted by the listener or reader when a short phrase is said in advance of the actual suggestion, to ease it into conversation or text. We refer to these small sentences as weasel or opening phrases.

It is unlikely you noticed, and such is the power of this technique, in the previous paragraph, the words, 'You will find when you'. This is a weasel phrase before the suggestion to 'use embedded commands', which is our intention. The rationale behind this illustration is to demonstrate just how easily ideas can be sneaked into text and conversation without the reader's or listener's conscious awareness.

Of course, merely writing a weasel phrase and a hidden suggestion does not make it a successful command; in written form it should be marked out in a manner that suits your style and the context in which it is being used: email, text message, brochure or sales letter. For example:

- You will find when you use embedded commands that the results, and so on.
- You will find when you *use embedded commands* that the results, and so on.
- You will find when you **use embedded commands** that the results, and so on.

In conversation, commands have to be delivered correctly; earlier we said the brain continuously searches for linguistic patterns and rhythmic speech, later we will show you how to achieve this, because this technique exploits this natural behaviour of our brains.

Once you have created a set of commands, start listening for opportunities to drop them into conversations and, in no time, you will begin, spontaneously, to form opening phrases within the context of your discussions. Weasel phrases are, nevertheless, the subject of much research. There follows a list of especially interesting opening sentences, with explanations as to how they may influence a listener. We have used each one to embed the commands 'read *Brilliant Persuasion*' and 'take part in a Proactive Persuasion Seminar'. Of course, you would use your own or refer to the examples given earlier in this chapter.

Opening phrase: When you

Example   When you *read Brilliant Persuasion,* you will realise how easy it is to become more persuasive.

Review   This phrase assumes the listener will do whatever you are proposing; it is not up for discussion.

Opening phrase: What would it be like if

Example   What would it be like if you *took part in a Proactive Persuasion Seminar* and won a massive deal within a few days and achieved your target for the quarter with nine weeks to go?

Review   This opening phrase is curious because it is also an embedded command. 'What would it be like if' is a question and another way of saying, 'Imagine,' we are indirectly directing our prospect to imagine whatever we suggest.

In this example, we are embedding the command 'take part in a Proactive Persuasion Seminar' while forming a question. We are also inviting the prospect to imagine how fantastic it will be to win a massive deal only days after taking part in the seminar.

Opening phrase: A person can

Example   A person can *read Brilliant Persuasion* and be
amazed at how quickly they will put into practice
the powerful techniques they have learnt.

Review   This is a fascinating opener because when we say 'A
person can', we deflect what follows away from our
subject, which has the effect of lowering potential
resistance, since we appear not to be talking or
referring to them.

Opening phrase: If you were to

Example   If you were to *read Brilliant Persuasion* you would
become so persuasive you might *request a salary
increase.*

Review   Similar to 'A person can', the word 'if' deflects
resistance and, again, creates the effect of leading
the listener on an imaginary journey.

The word 'if' also removes resistance and is followed
by the command 'read *Brilliant Persuasion*', then
another weasel phrase follows, ending with the resistance deflector 'might', which gently leads to a second
suggestion, 'request a salary increase'. This is very
powerful.

Opening phrase: As you

Example   As you *read Brilliant Persuasion,* you will discover
what it feels like to be so much more *successful.*

Review   This phrase is similar to 'When you' because it
assumes your prospect will act directly upon your
request.

In addition to the command, we have emphasised the word 'successful' because it is a positive feeling that we want the prospect to enjoy.

Opening phrase: You might find

Example   You might find when you *take part in a Proactive Persuasion Seminar* that your level of self-confidence grows as you regularly win more new business.

Review   When using this phrase, we are implying that our prospects are going to encounter what we portray as something that naturally happens.

Opening phrase: To the point where

Example   You might find as you *read Brilliant Persuasion*, that you will get to the point where you will *feel confident* enough to *find a bigger challenge.*

Review   This opener links one thing your prospect is experiencing to another.

In this example, the suggestion 'read *Brilliant Persuasion*' precedes the command to 'feel confident'. It is always a good idea to combine what you want someone to do with a positive emotional state. We have added a further command to 'find a bigger challenge'. Who knows? You might!

Opening phrase: Invite you to notice

Example   And I invite you to notice when you *take part in a Proactive Persuasion Seminar,* that you will be able to build stronger, more lucrative client relationships.

Review   This is similar to 'you might find' because, again, we are implying that what we portray is something that naturally happens. The word 'invite' has congenial associations, suggesting any actions taken are done so freely.

Opening phrase: How surprised would you be

Example   How surprised would you be to *read Brilliant Persuasion* and discover you are already using some of the techniques described in the book and did not realise?

Review   It is implicit that your suggestion will occur; the only uncertainty is how astounded they will be when it does.

Weasel phrases that lower resistance and increase responsiveness by redirection

To lower resistance, improve responsiveness and reassure your prospect you are not pressing or compelling them to act on anything you might say, even though you are, we use negation statements. These are ingenious because they effectively take the edge off the command by redirecting the conscious attention of the listener.

**Opening phrase: There is no need to/It is not
                  necessary to**

Example   There is no need to *take part in a Proactive Persuasion Seminar* if you want to become more persuasive.

Review   This is a superb opening phrase because it is a resistance eliminator. We begin by suggesting you do not have to do something and then, immediately, the opposite message of 'need to take part in a Proactive Persuasion Seminar if you want to be more persuasive' is delivered subliminally in command form.

Opening phrase: You really shouldn't

Example   You really shouldn't *read Brilliant Persuasion* if you don't need to *make more money*.

Review   Again, we are informing our prospect that
          they really should not act upon what we are
          about to say. Negation statements, like these,
          initially might sound odd and counterintuitive.
          However, remember, the most important phrase
          in the sentence is the embedded command. The
          subconscious mind assimilates the positive; it
          cannot make sense of the negative statement.

          Appreciating the psychology of negation, you can
          spot both messages above: 'read *Brilliant Persuasion*'
          and 'make more money'.

---

brilliant action

Think about this. What is the most important factor to you about having
more money? Make a list, either in your mind or, better still, take a moment
and write it down. Be honest and make it truly personal and, if possible, prepare yours before reviewing ours.

- Build your confidence.
- Make you feel happier.
- Gain more respect from your colleagues.
- Show the world how successful you are.
- Enjoy more exotic holidays abroad.
- Pay off all your debt.
- Buy a bigger house or car.
- Spend more time with the family.
- Enjoy financial independence.
- Greater personal freedom.

It is possible you either thought about or wrote something down from
this list. Ultimately, we suspect greater personal freedom is something
many of us seek. With that in mind:

▶

You really shouldn't *read Brilliant Persuasion* if you do not want to *enjoy greater personal freedom.*

That is a very powerful statement, isn't it? Who does not want more personal freedom to live their lives exactly how they wish? Negation statements, such as, 'really shouldn't', 'don't want', and 'There is no need to' help us to persuade, by appearing to remove resistance and facilitate the use of thought-provoking suggestions.

Opening phrase: Don't

Example   Don't decide to *read Brilliant Persuasion* today until . . .

Review   Similar to 'shouldn't', 'don't' appears to direct more fervently your prospects not to do something or act in a particular manner.

Once again, contingent upon how this is delivered, the subconscious mind, being unable to detect the negative, picks up 'decide to read *Brilliant Persuasion* today'.

---

brilliant example

Have you ever heard a parent or carer say to a child 'Don't hit your brother like that'? As we reveal more of how the subconscious mind accepts only positive information, depending upon how this request is delivered, now you will appreciate that the child is really receiving a command to hit his or her brother, the exact opposite of the intention. Similarly, how often have you heard, 'Don't forget your keys'? Again, the subliminal suggestion is 'Forget your keys'.

Opening phrase: If

Example   If you *read Brilliant Persuasion* now, I can assure you
that . . .

Review   Contrary to conventional sales training, suggesting
that the word 'if' installs doubt and weakens
sales presentations, remember it is the command/
suggestion following the word 'if' that is the most
important.

Using 'if' appears to give a choice to the listener,
implying they can 'if' they wish. When persuading or
negotiating with others, consider 'if' as a very useful
word, enabling the almost effortless delivery of powerful commands and suggestions, like these:

- If you *agree now* . . .
- If you *sign up* now . . .
- *If, like me,* you can imagine . . .
- If you *consider this* . . .
- If you *call me* at . . .
- *If you want this* to . . .

The *weasel* or *opening phrases* we have just covered are:

- A person can . . .
- If you were to . . .
- As you . . .
- You might find . . .
- To the point where . . .
- Invite you to notice . . .
- How surprised would you be?
- When you . . .

The *redirection* and *negation phrases* were:

- If . . .
- Don't . . .
- You really shouldn't . . .
- It is not necessary to . . .

It is important to be flexible when you start to use weasel phrases. Some students like to remember them all, while others prefer to use the concept as a reason not to use embedded commands often. All the listed opening phrases are optional because, as we mentioned earlier, as you prepare commands, you will, intuitively, form weasel phrases within the context of your discussions; they will just happen, effortlessly.

How many embedded commands are there in the above paragraph?

- Be flexible.
- Use weasel phrases.
- Remember them all.
- Use embedded commands often.
- Prepare commands.

Are there more?

How to deliver embedded commands in conversation – influencing the subconscious

When expressing embedded commands, it is important to pay careful attention to your tone of voice, timing and the rhythm of your speech.

There are three steps to follow when articulating embedded commands:

Step 1   Speak in your usual manner and speed and
           introduce your weasel phrase, and then *pause*
           for a second.

Step 2   Following the first pause, state your command as you lower your voice slightly at the same time. By doing this, you will appear in control, professionally authoritative and confident. Then *pause* for a second.

Step 3   Following your second pause, continue the conversation in your usual style.

Follow this pattern:

Weasel or opening phrase + pause + command, using slight downward inflection + pause + continue the conversation as normal.

brilliant tips

- It is imperative to be confident when you use embedded commands. Always use a downward commanding inflection and pause in the right places. If you do not, you will find that, once you start to add commands into speech, they will not work because you will appear to be asking questions and/or indicating uncertainty.

- Pausing for short periods may, initially, feel unnatural until you can relax when you deliver commands. Remember, your prospect believes this is how you usually talk and, of course, it will be, as you practise daily.

exercise 1

Below we have marked out the embedded commands that appear in the previous Brilliant tip, using two methods. We have signified a brief pause in speech with three dots '...' and have italicised the commands.

1   A pause is signified by '...'.

2   Commands are *italicised*.

Now read out loud the following paragraph, pausing when you see this '. . .' and use a downward inflection and a slightly deeper commanding tone of voice when the text is italicised.

- It is imperative to . . . *be confident* . . . when you . . . *use embedded commands* . . . Always use a downward commanding inflection and pause in the right places. If you do not, you will find that, once you . . . *start to add commands* . . . into speech, they will not work because you will appear to be asking questions and/or indicating uncertainty.

- Pausing for short periods may, initially, feel unnatural until . . . *you can relax* . . . when you deliver commands. Remember, your prospect believes this is how you usually talk and, of course, it will be, as you . . . *practise daily.*

The commands are:

- Be confident.
- Use embedded commands.
- Start to add commands.
- Add commands into speech.
- You can relax.
- Relax when you deliver commands.
- Practise daily.

If you were to refer to the original Brilliant tip, you would realise, if you have not already done so, that the spacing before and after each command is slightly larger. If you did not notice this consciously, your subconscious brain picked it up and started to work on the suggestions. Review this chapter to this point for other commands similarly marked out.

It is worth stating that some people feel enthusiastic when they begin to use this subliminal form of communication. With time and a little practice, most people who have adopted it have felt that it produced the results they wanted and found that their prospects believed it was their natural way of talking.

In the earlier Brilliant tip, instead of saying, 'It is important to . . . be confident . . . when you . . . use embedded commands' what if we had said 'When you embed commands, do not worry if you think you sound strange because your prospect will believe this is your natural speaking voice'?

What messages hide in this apparently harmless statement that is representative of how most people speak? The subliminal suggestions are exactly the opposite of the intended message; they are, 'worry' and 'you sound strange'.

brilliant tip

Enhance your communication skills by saying precisely what you mean in an unambiguous manner, closed to interpretation by the subconscious minds of others.

Embedding commands – the dispersal technique

Up until this point, we have described embedded commands as short statements of up to four or five words, which include an action verb. There is another method often used to deliver subliminal messages; it takes a little more preparation and entails creating and remembering short scripts.

This technique is known as the dispersal technique because we distribute suggestions within a short story in a manner that influences the subconscious mind of your prospects.

Read this out loud:

I recall a prospective client once enquired if we could undertake a salary survey. I said, 'Jim,' we were on first name terms, 'I will make some initial telephone inquiries and call you next week.' Our brief was to include firms in Continental Europe. My company at that time was Stephen St James & Associates and we had a strong network in Europe we could approach. Our focus was to be limited to Northern Europe, as the client preferred the Swedish, Danish, French and German suppliers, who most closely matched their own corporate profile. Somehow, it was different in Southern Europe. Quickly, we assembled a list of the target companies we proposed to approach. The prospect was delighted when I called back, and we were formally appointed to undertake the assignment.

Now, read it again, out loud, pausing for a second when you see this '. . .' and accentuating the italicised words with a lower commanding tone of voice. Notice how the suggestion is gradually revealed.

I recall a prospective client once enquired if we could undertake a salary survey. I said, 'Jim,' we were on first name terms, . . . '*I will* . . . make some initial telephone inquiries and call you next week.' Our brief was to . . . *include* . . . firms in Continental Europe. My company at that time was . . . *Stephen St James &* *Associates* . . . and we had a strong network . . . *in* . . . Europe we could approach. . . . *Our* . . . focus was to be limited to Northern Europe, as the client . . . *preferred* . . . the Swedish, Danish, French and German . . . *suppliers* . . . who most closely matched their own corporate profile. Somehow, it was different in Southern Europe. Quickly, we assembled a . . . *list* . . . of the target companies we proposed to approach. The prospect was delighted when I called back, and we were formally appointed to undertake the assignment.

The actual message we wish to relay is now evident. Still, keep practising reading to acquaint yourself with pausing and varying your tone of voice. This works because the subconscious brain is constantly looking for linguistic patterns and rhythm and only it detects the emphasised words, while the conscious mind is interested only in the bigger story.

Your task is to list the suggestions you want to convey and integrate them into your presentation, then, when talking with your prospect, adopt the three-step system covered earlier to deliver your presentation and emphasise the core message.

brilliant tips

- The 'carrier story' is the bigger story carrying your suggestions and can be about any subject of your choosing. For example, if you know your prospect had recently returned from a holiday in a place you have visited, as you engage in general conversation *before* your main presentation, relay your carrier story containing your suggestions about a similar holiday or an airport experience. If you do not have a story, *make one up!*

- Experiment by integrating appropriate generic suggestions into your carrier stories about general life events.

- Review articles in newspapers and trade journals and rewrite them to include your suggestions and commit them to memory.

Some final words about practising embedding commands:

- Experiment with both direct and dispersed commands in a non-pressurised environment.
- Speak slowly and, as your confidence increases, gradually build up speed.
- Exaggerate lowering the tone of your voice and pausing between normal sentences and commands.

With determination and practice, your tonal changes and short pauses will become subtle and almost imperceptible.

Use the information you have acquired in this section carefully. Have fun embedding commands!

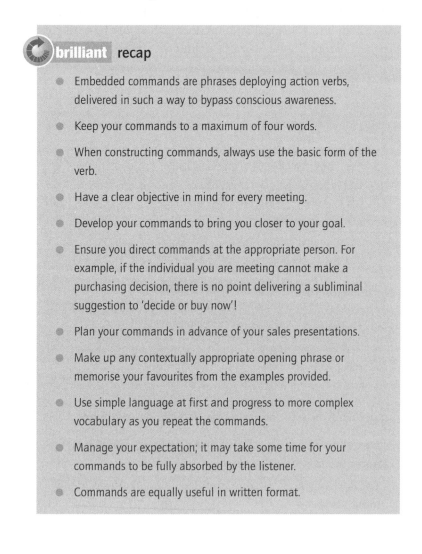

brilliant recap

- Embedded commands are phrases deploying action verbs, delivered in such a way to bypass conscious awareness.

- Keep your commands to a maximum of four words.

- When constructing commands, always use the basic form of the verb.

- Have a clear objective in mind for every meeting.

- Develop your commands to bring you closer to your goal.

- Ensure you direct commands at the appropriate person. For example, if the individual you are meeting cannot make a purchasing decision, there is no point delivering a subliminal suggestion to 'decide or buy now'!

- Plan your commands in advance of your sales presentations.

- Make up any contextually appropriate opening phrase or memorise your favourites from the examples provided.

- Use simple language at first and progress to more complex vocabulary as you repeat the commands.

- Manage your expectation; it may take some time for your commands to be fully absorbed by the listener.

- Commands are equally useful in written format.

PART 2

Persuasive language patterns

CHAPTER 2

The redefine

Easily resolve objections and lead sales conversations towards your goal

'When obstacles arise, you change your direction to reach your goal; you do not change your decision to get there.'

Zig Ziglar

W hat is it like when you realise you have lost the lead position in a conversation and had to backtrack, or an unanticipated idea is introduced, entirely shifting the game plan? Worse still, when someone interjects and challenges you just as you have psyched yourself up and launched into an especially important presentation, severely disrupting your flow precisely at the wrong time?

Alternatively, have you ever experienced an occasion when you were unable to think on your feet quickly enough as objections fly your way during a business meeting? Maybe you are the person who prefers to allow others to take the reigns, not because you cannot, of course, it is just there never appears to be an opportunity for you to express your view and, besides, others seem to take control more readily.

Incidents such as these have happened to most professional sales marketeers at some point in their careers, haven't they? If you have experienced any of these situations, in this chapter you are going to discover a sophisticated way to recover your position and retake control of any conversation and never find yourself deferring to others. You will be able to draw the subject back to what is important to you and respond to any objection and, most importantly, ensure others follow *your* lead.

The ingenious language pattern you are about to learn is called *the redefine*. I agree its title appears somewhat technical, and I would add the issue is not about the name of the technique you are going to discover, the issue is how quickly you will be empowered by the significant, persuasive and conversational advantage you will acquire. Ask yourself how important it is to be able to eloquently and seamlessly lead conversations directly towards your objectives. To not have to defer to colleagues or be thrown off course by the unexpected challenges of others.

The purpose of the redefine is to enable you to gracefully and efficiently:

● change the direction or subject of a conversation towards issues, events and ideas important to *you*!

● grab back and take control of a discussion or debate;

● modify the way a person might think about something or change their minds completely;

● have the answer to any sales objection;

● never be flummoxed by anyone during a business meeting;

● have the confidence to express your view, not always deferring to others.

How redefining works when an objection is presented

The redefine has two parts: part one – when someone expresses an objection, your first task is to repeat it, stating the issue is not whatever he or she has just said, then move the conversation forwards by saying what the real issue is; this is your goal or at least a step closer towards it.

Once you have replaced what they have said with the real issue (your goal), inform the listener(s) what this means, and you can decide whatever you want it to mean as long as it brings the conversation closer towards the outcome you seek. In the second part, an optional element of the redefine, we ask a question, essentially funnelling the thoughts of the listener closer towards your point of view.

The structure of the redefine

Where (A) represents the other person's viewpoint or stated objection and (B) denotes the topic you wish to introduce, continue with 'and that means this' or 'and this means that'.

Part one   The issue is not (A) the issue is (B) and that means . . . or and this means that . . .

After saying either 'This means that' or 'That means This', the fun begins because it can *mean* anything of your choosing, as long as the overall objective of realigning the conversation towards your outcome is accomplished.

Part two Asking a question

In the second, and optional, part of this pattern, we advocate asking a question. For many students of persuasion, part one is sufficient and, in most teachings on this subject, there is no part two. However, we favour the idea of asking a question principally because it allows us to plant suggestions and unequivocally focus the mind of our antagonist(s) firmly on our goal.

Should you choose to follow the redefine with a question, keep in mind, the most compelling questions always begin with the words, 'what', 'how' and 'where'. Asking questions starting with these words ensures the listener has to think seriously about the new subject you are introducing into the conversation, and, at the same time, prevents them from answering with a single word.

brilliant tip

If you decide to ask a question after the redefine, always separate the redefine from the question with the word 'and' like this:

The issue isn't (A) the issue is (B), *and* I'm wondering, what's your view on (subject related to 'B')

To maximise your results, follow this question format:

The redefine + *And*	I am/we are	wondering	What, How,
		Curious to learn	Where
		Interested to understand	

You would not say:

● The issue is not X, the issue is Y. But, tell me, I'm wondering what. . . and so on.

Again, the word 'But' subliminally negates, in the listener's mind, everything preceding it. In this example, crucially, the subject to which you have redirected the conversation is annulled in favour of the question and weakens the power of the pattern.

brilliant tips

The words 'and' and 'but' dynamically influence, and can even entirely reverse, the expected meaning of sentences and questions.

● When using the redefine, always say '*and* this means that' or '*and* that means this'.

● On no account say, ' *but* this means' or '*but* that means' because this subliminally negates in the mind of the listener everything that precedes it.

● Should you choose to ask a question after the redefine, always separate the end of the redefine and the beginning of your question with the word 'and'.

Pattern overview options

● The issue is not (A), the issue is (B) and that means (C).

● The issue is not (A), the issue is (B) and that means (C) (*any word other than but*): I am/we are wondering/curious/ interested + what, how or where.

- The issue is not (A), the issue is (B) *and* I am/we are wondering/curious/interested + what, how or where.

▶ brilliant examples

Example 1

I remember, in the late 1970s, as a junior advertising sales executive, meeting a new prospect. After the preliminaries, he said, 'I am meeting you as a courtesy. We don't advertise, as all our business comes via word of mouth, times are good.'

I immediately had an answer for this objection or buying signal, even though I was unaware my response was a language pattern, a pattern I have used time and time again with great success. You, like me, may be the same, and not know when you instinctively use language patterns.

Much later in life, I recognised language patterns in my speech and proactively used them throughout my career in sales and, of course, instantly realised when others used them on me. This is a significant bonus you will enjoy.

I looked at the prospect and said, 'I agree. Business looks good. The issue is not that all your business comes via word of mouth, the issue is that, if you have never advertised, you have never experienced how much more business you will achieve with a regular campaign. And that means I am curious. Tell me what's important to you about increasing your month-on-month sales and raising your revenues?

Example 2

Last year, I presented a Proactive Persuasion Seminar and workshop to a group of recruiters. As part of the presentation, I invite delegates to present their most challenging objections. Attending the event was one of the company's directors. He was struggling to convince a prospect to retain his business on a contingency basis.

The objection was, indeed, quite challenging and insurmountable for him at that time. As an executive search professional (headhunter), he had

▶

poached almost all of the best managers from his desired future client. The managing director knew he had done this and expressed an objection to him personally and professionally for removing his best people. As an executive search consultant in a previous life, it is a situation my team and I encountered occasionally, I introduced them to the redefine, as it is a perfect solution.

The response we proposed was along these lines:

I agree; you know I have systematically removed your key managers over a period of six months. However, the issue is not that I took your key people, the most important issue is that, when we work together now, you know how tenacious I am. That I'll stop at nothing to get the best people for my clients and how I never accept no for an answer. I'll work like that for you. What advantages can you imagine you'll benefit from to have an acknowledged industry specialist like me on your side?

After presenting this solution, it was reworded to suit the communication style of the delegate, who left the room. Later in the day, I was informed he had won the assignment with this once unyielding prospect.

I wonder if you have already realised, as you become more proactively persuasive, how important it is to be confident with your vocabulary. Curiously, then, the issue is not whether you are comfortable with the new persuasive terminology you are learning, the issue is to maintain your personal communication style and to benefit from the power of this technique while mirroring the structure of the pattern.

There follows an assortment of alternative ways of expressing the Redefine. Use them if you are comfortable with the language or, better still, make up your own while rigorously adhering to the format of the pattern:

- I see. Only (A) is not the most important point. The most important aspect is (B) and that means we should (C). What do you imagine is . . . ?

- The weakness in your argument is not so much to do with (A). The area requiring more brainstorming is (B) and this means that (C). What areas can you . . . ?

- The point is not (A), but it is (B) and this means (C). How do you propose we . . . ?

- The question is not about (A), it is about (B) and that means when is the best time for you to . . . ?

brilliant tips

- It is imperative, whether you are negotiating or aiming to convince someone, to know your desired outcome from the outset. If you do not have a definitive result in mind, it will be impossible to measure your effectiveness. The outcome need not be your ultimate goal.

- Practise saying this pattern out loud as often as possible. Look at yourself in a mirror as you speak, observe how your facial expression changes as you say the words. Make up theoretical objections and respond to them out loud. If you prefer to replace the word 'issue', use your words and always follow the structure of the pattern.

- One of the best ways to embed language patterns into your everyday conversation is to find a like-minded colleague and practise together daily and have fun.

brilliant recap

Use the redefine to:

- change the way someone thinks about something;
- respond to objections;

▶

- direct conversations closer towards your goal;
- grab back conversations, should they become irrelevant to your objective;
- change the topic of a conversation;
- get others on-board with your direction of thought.

Recommendations:

- Fashion your vocabulary around the core format of the pattern.
- Create some hypothetical client/prospect conversations where you can use the redefine and recite your response out loud to familiarise yourself, expressing your words within the structure of the pattern.

Now you are aware of this pattern, use it to respond to objections and redirect any conversation closer towards your objective.

CHAPTER 3

The agreement frame

Naturally remove resistance, increase rapport and counter any objection

'I always say "I couldn't agree more", even if I wholeheartedly disagree, because whether I completely agree or completely disagree, I couldn't agree more.'

Jarod Kintz

an you recall the last time you were in agreement with your client or prospect, when you expressed the same opinion as them? Did you have a sense this feeling of accord influenced them sufficiently enough that they wanted to purchase your goods? Were you even deliberately attempting to do this at that time?

Most people do not, generally, consider agreement as a method of persuasion. You likely agreed with your prospect's point of view because you did and nothing more! I agree, that may sound obvious, and I would like to add that this is, indeed, how most people think about agreement.

In this chapter, we discuss the effect that just appearing to agree engenders in others, and how to *actively* use this to increase rapport, remove resistance and raise responsiveness. We introduce a linguistic pattern, a combination of words that takes advantage of the agreement effect and enables us to subtly redirect and control conversations, bringing them closer towards our objective, and we explore how to flip objections into positive reasons to buy.

Before we describe how to prepare and use the agreement frame, let us first make clear what we mean by the word 'frame' in this particular context. The term 'frame' defines the boundaries around a conversation or an experience and, in this chapter, we are discussing the experience of agreement.

Having described frames, let us return to the agreement frame and discuss what it is and why it is so powerful. 'I agree' is something most of us say every day and have little idea that it forms part of a tiny, yet significant, language pattern. It becomes a dynamic, persuasive technique once we appreciate the effect the words 'I agree' have on others and how we choose to use this insight to create the outcomes you seek.

Think about these questions for a moment:

- How do you feel when someone agrees with you?
- How do you feel about the person agreeing with you?
- What often occurs conversationally when someone agrees with you?

Now answer these questions:

- How do you feel when someone disagrees with you?
- How do you feel about the person disagreeing with you?
- What can sometimes happen conversationally when someone disagrees with you?

When others disagree with us, very often, we are immediately on our guard and, as we persevere to make our case, the conversation may become more clinical and, occasionally, depending on the context, it may cease altogether, and rapport subsides as both parties agree to disagree.

Conversely, can you remember how you felt when one of your colleagues agreed with something you said? We like it when others agree with us, don't we? It is human nature. Have you noticed once you say to someone, 'I agree' or 'You're right' that, usually, they instinctively continue speaking, offering more information? This happens because they have not detected any resistance to their line of communication. You are going to take advantage of this aspect of human nature to strengthen your persuasive abilities.

> ### brilliant tip
>
> An effective way to remove resistance and build rapport with your prospect is to agree or *appear* to agree with their point of view. Whatever it is, even if we disagree!

How to agree with the disagreeable

Without being entirely unethical, we do not even have to subscribe wholly to our prospect's viewpoint when we use the agreement frame.

Should something be said that you really cannot accept under any circumstances, it is still possible to enjoy the benefits of the agreement frame effect by saying:

- I can agree with part of what you've said *and* . . .
- It is possible at some point I might agree with that *and* . . .
- I agree you said that *and* . . .
- I almost agree with that and . . .

By intentionally using this pattern, you have chosen to agree with your prospect to deliberately increase their responsiveness. You will appear aligned to their way of thinking. They will sense this and, as you notice their resistance lowering, you assume control of the conversation and steer it towards your goal.

Review the following statements:

Prospect:	**Persuader:**
We do not need this now	I agree. You're right. It's entirely possible. You don't need this now *and* . . .

It is not really what we want	I agree you have said that *and* . . .
It is just too expensive	Yes, you are right. I agree. It has a higher value in the market *and* . . .
I have not got time	I agree time is precious *and* . . .

I can imagine you thinking how incomprehensible it is to agree with these objections and, guess what? I agree you might believe that, and that is why everything will become clear once we examine the structure of this response.

The agreement frame pattern structure

The agreement frame pattern has three stages and we look at each one in turn.

Stage one

Your chosen form of agreement statement followed by the word 'and'. (This list is for guidance only. Use whatever form of agreement most fits your communication style.)

- I agree you are right *and* . . .
- I agree *and* . . .
- I could not have said that better myself *and* . . .
- You took the words out of my mouth *and* . . .
- Yes, perfect. You are right as usual *and* . . .
- I respect your point of view *and* . . .
- I agree you might think/have thought that *and* . . .
- I appreciate your stance *and* . . .
- I recognise the value of what you are saying/have said *and* . . .
- I could not agree more *and* . . .
- You're quite right *and* . . .
- Maybe you're right *and* . . .

brilliant tip

When using the agreement frame to counteract objections, it is most effective to express your response in the past tense. This will not be perceived by your prospect, however, on a subconscious level, it effectively makes the doubt historic. For example, 'I recognise the value of what you have *said* and . . .' or 'I agree you might have *thought* that and . . .'

Stage two

A linking phrase:

- I would add/I would like to add . . .
- That means this . . . this means that . . .
- That is why . . .

Stage three

Reintroduce into the conversation the subject that is important to you, thus steering it towards your objective.

brilliant recap

The structure of the agreement frame is:

Agreement Statement + And + Linking phrase + Redirect conversation to subject of your choice

How to reinforce a sense of agreement

One of the most powerful and little-taught techniques to reinforce agreement is to proactively incorporate body language into your presentations. Look your prospect in the eyes and, while stating your agreement phrase, slowly nod your head three times. This has the effect of further deepening rapport and convinces your prospect you are on their side.

brilliant tips

● Always use 'and' to separate the two parts of the agreement pattern, because 'and' continues the flow of the conversation and leads your prospect from where they currently are towards where you want them to be.

● Try to avoid using the term 'I understand' as an agreement statement because it is quite difficult to understand anyone. It is far easier to agree with others rather than to profess to understand them.

brilliant action

Listen to political debates on the radio or television and notice how often professional politicians use agreement to lead the interview towards the specific areas they wish to discuss.

Recently, enjoying my daily fix of the morning news, a presenter, well-known for his no-nonsense and rather forthright interviewing style, was interviewing a senior politician who had just given a rather oblique answer to his first question; unhappy with the response, the presenter continued with:

Presenter   Nobody would argue with that (pause while politician continued to speak) *and* the question is . . . ?'

This is an excellent example of a modified agreement statement, 'nobody would argue with that' is another way of saying 'everyone agrees'. Whether anyone would or not is irrelevant. Then, leading the conversation by saying, '*and* the question is . . . ?' The message in this example is to be confident using your own style of agreement and adhere to the structure of the pattern.

Agreement and reframing

To further elevate your powers of persuasion, combine the agreement frame with reframing. This will afford you an unstoppable ability to counter most objections.

When we reframe, we take a prospect's objection and repeat it from a positive perspective. Mastering this requires a little preparation. A good starting point is to list the aspect of your product, service and/or company that receives most objections. If necessary, have a brainstorming session with your colleagues. Once you have a list of objections, turn each one on its head and express it positively using the following Reframe pattern.

The Reframe pattern structure

Where X is the negative statement about your product/service and Y represents how you have converted it into a sales advantage. For our example, we will use a price objection.

● The issue is not about X. The issue is about Y. Continue with 'and that means' or ask a question.

After practising flipping the negatives into positives, add the agreement frame to the front of the reframe. The pattern looks like this:

Agreement statement + *and* + I would add + reframed negative statement + A question.

The complete response is as follows:

Well, thank you for your honesty. I have to say I agree how you might have thought that pricing was high and I would say, having listened to what you've said, the issue seems not to be about the price. The most important issue is about quality, isn't it? What's the most significant benefit your company will enjoy by using higher quality products?

brilliant recap

- The agreement frame will not work if the words 'but/however/ yet' separate Stage one and Stage two.

- Use only the word 'and' to separate stages one and two of the pattern to maintain the forward movement of the conversation and lead your subject towards your goal.

- 'I understand' tends to be avoided as an agreement statement.

- Listen for this pattern on television and radio talk shows.

- Practise agreeing with everything anyone says and observe their response.

- Practise disagreeing with others and notice how the response differs.

- Nod your head three times as you say an agreement statement (do not overuse this technique).

- Follow this pattern: agreement phrase and head nod + *and* + linking phrase + topic of your choosing.

CHAPTER 4

Linguistic mathematics

Subconsciously add and delete thoughts and create positive emotions in the minds of others

'You can't imagine just how much believing in negative thoughts is affecting your life . . . until you stop.'

Charles F. Glassman

n this chapter, we reveal how most people unknowingly subliminally transmit negative messages and feelings to others by misusing two small, simple English words. Our particular goal is to ensure you correctly apply these words when giving feedback and overcoming objections and to make sure that you consistently leave positive feelings in the minds of your prospects and clients.

Embedding constructive messages and developing positive feelings about you in the subconscious minds of others will ensure they are confident and upbeat about you and enjoy being in your company. This, in turn, deepens rapport, removes resistance and enhances your status.

This chapter titled 'linguistic mathematics' refers to the conjunctions 'and' and 'but', which all too often are swapped around, despite having opposing implications for whatever is said before them. The word 'but' not only casts doubt, it effectively negates ideas and sentiments that precede it. For this reason, we will represent it with a (−) sign. Conversely, the word 'and' sustains and supports everything said before it, and links statements and language patterns that follow it and is denoted by a (+) sign, hence linguistic mathematics!

It is hard to believe how words so small wield such influence. These seemingly inconsequential, often misused, language patterns, when correctly deployed, are unexpectedly powerful and not to be underestimated. We focus on using them to:

- give negative feedback or bad news;
- annihilate objections.

brilliant tip

Learn to acknowledge and draw upon the persuasive and influential properties your vocabulary has on the subconscious minds of others. It is unlikely your prospects or clients have the aptitude to pinpoint or verbalise exactly why they enjoy working with, purchasing from or feeling more comfortable with one individual over another. The subliminal emotional responses you can actively trigger in others by using appropriate vocabulary is fundamental to engendering positive working relationships.

How to deliver negative feedback or bad news

The most important rule to follow when providing bad news, negative feedback or, if you are called upon to express an unfavourable opinion or assessment about something, is always to say the negative statement about the subject first and follow this with the word 'but' and, finally, state the good news.

Pattern structure 1

Bad news + but + good news

By giving feedback like this, the initial negative statement is both softened and subliminally negated when followed by the word 'but'. The final part of the message the listener hears is the good news, which appeals to them on a conscious level and subconsciously embeds positive feelings in their minds about you and the products and services you are promoting.

🔘 brilliant examples

Example 1

An advertising agency team manager arranges a brainstorming session to identify solutions for an especially testing situation with one of their clients. An account manager presents some innovative suggestions and the team manager responds with:

Response 1   Some good ideas there and possibly worth trying *but* it's unlikely the client will agree to that plan.

Analysis   In direct opposition to the fundamental rule of persuasion this reply credits the good ideas first, then instantly negates them by the incorrect placement of the word 'but', effectively saying, 'I like your ideas, but not really.'

Or

Response 2   I am unsure whether the customer will accept that plan, *but* your ideas are sound and possibly worth trying.

Analysis   Following the pattern precisely, in this instance the word 'but' correctly negates the uncertainty the client may have about the approach, then positively acknowledges the ideas presented by the account manager leaving him/her feeling appreciated.

The above example is a team management scenario and the manager, aware of the impact of language, can effectively choose the mood of the team. The manager, unaware of the impact language, may, potentially, permanently struggle by unknowingly giving opposing subliminal messages to those with whom he/she works.

Example 2

A recruitment consultant, without a shortlist, is summoned to his/her client to deliver a timely progress report concerning a current assignment. He/she might say:

▶

Response 1   The candidates we've identified look good on paper, but we have not secured a shortlist.

Analysis   Opposing the rule of always giving negative feedback first, the recruitment consultant indicates that the candidates identified on paper look strong and immediately proceeds to negate this good news with the incorrect placement of the word 'but'. The final message left with the client is certainly one that will heighten anxiety.

Or

Response 2   We have not secured a shortlist *yet,* but the candidates we have identified look good on paper.

Analysis   The absence of a suitable shortlist is negated immediately by the correct placement of the word 'but'. The final message left with the client confirms the existence of strong candidates in the pipeline. Use of the word 'yet' adds movement to a seemingly static situation and progress appears implicit.

In the second example, the client is confident their assignment is progressing and, perhaps most importantly, they are in no doubt their choice of recruitment consultancy is a good one, even though the same feedback was given in both scenarios.

How to intensify this language pattern

When we require greater control over a conversation and need to lead it decisively towards our objectives, to talk about what is important to us and further our cause, we can strengthen this pattern simply by adding the word 'and'.

Pattern structure 2

Bad news + but + good news + *and*

The inclusion of the word 'and' at the end of the pattern allows us to introduce new subjects or ideas and redirect a conversation towards any areas of our choosing, drawing it closer towards our objectives. Returning to our earlier example responses:

Advertising agency manager:

> *Response*   I am unsure whether the customer will accept that plan, *but* your ideas are sound and possibly worth trying
>
> *and*
>
> I am going to bring Jane to our team because she has an inspired approach and will be a welcome addition to the team.

Recruitment consultant:

> *Response*   We have not secured a shortlist yet, but the candidates we have identified on paper are strong,
>
> *and*
>
> you mentioned earlier that your commercial director was considering early retirement. What would you like us to do to find his replacement?

Scorpion compliments

How many times have you overheard someone give a scorpion compliment or have you been on the receiving end of one? Here are a few examples:

- Well done! Excellent sales skills winning that deal, but a shame there's no way you'll get close to your quarterly target.

- You've done a great job getting that report finished, but it's a pity about the spelling mistakes.

- You cooked a great meal, thank you, but just a little too much fat for us.

- That's a great proposal document, but still lacks the detail we need.

- The properties you've shown us look excellent, but you've still not quite grasped exactly what we are seeking.

- The website you've designed has visual impact, but the colours are not exactly our corporate style.

All these compliments have a sting in their tail, hence the scorpion compliment.

brilliant action

- For the next three days, experiment with replacing the word *but* with *and* – and notice the impact this has on others.

- Actively listen to conversations and spot how many times you hear others genuinely giving compliments then negating them.

How to annihilate objections

The information you now have will equip you to use a brilliant technique that turns any objection into definite reasons why your prospect should buy your product or service. We challenged you to listen to others unknowingly misusing the word 'but'. Now we are going to introduce a linguistic technique that ensures you will always have the perfect response to anyone who poses an objection to your products or services, using the word 'but'.

The objection reversal technique

The objection reversal technique is quite crafty, and you will use it in almost every conversation with a prospect. Remember, your obligation is to assist your prospect to reverse their negativity by refocusing them towards the positive aspects of your offering and, in so doing, reaffirming the reasons why they should buy.

The pattern structure

> Agreement + reason for objection + but + confirm desire
> + because + specific benefits + tag question + solution

This is a very simple technique, so let us concentrate on carefully analysing and describing the purpose of each element of the pattern.

Element	Description
Agreement	It is a good idea to acquire the habit of agreeing with your prospects when they object to any part of your presentation. It has the effect of momentarily disarming them. The lack of resistance from you to their objection lulls them into a feeling of security; they are unaware of the language patterns you are about to bring into play to reverse their train of thought. All you have to say is, 'I agree', 'You are right', 'That's correct. I agree' or, maybe, 'I agree with part of what you have said/I agree you have said that.' However, you express agreement in your words.
Objection	Restate their objection *using their exact words*. They will relate to it better, and it signals you have actively listened and respected their point of view.
But	Now subliminally remove the objection by using the word 'but'.

Confirm desire	It is likely that a prospect will like a part of your product. Reaffirm these points.
Because	We use the word 'because', as it connects both parts of the response together and smoothly leads the conversation forwards towards emphasising a selection of specific benefits. ('The reason you want this is *because* you'll enjoy A, B and C.')
	The word 'because' is a language pattern on its own. From childhood it is ingrained in us to accept that whatever follows is a suitable explanation for whatever precedes it.
Tag question	This is a little question like: Wouldn't you? Couldn't you? Won't it? Haven't you? We add these at the end of sentences to elicit either an audible or inaudible 'yes' response. If you nod your head a couple of times when you ask a tag question, it makes it visually compelling, too. Do not nod too often, though, for obvious reasons!
Solution	However you define this in the context of your meeting.

Let's review some examples using the objection reversal technique.

🔵 **brilliant** examples

Example 1

Prospect   I'd like to own your product, but it is too expensive.

Persuader   I agree, it is expensive *but* you'd like to own it *because* you can see how it will make a huge difference in your life. You'll be able to A, B and C, won't you? So let's work out how we can achieve this together.

Example 2

Prospect   Looks interesting, but I have no time to discuss this.

Persuader   Clearly, you are busy and I agree it appears you have no time right now, *but* you can see this looks interesting *because* it is going to enable you to A, B and C, isn't it?

(Follow through by coordinating diaries.)

Naively, your prospect believes they have ended the conversation after the word 'but'. To their astonishment, you cleverly reverse their response and use 'but' to negate their objection. You proceed by saying 'because', then reintroduce all the benefits and clear-cut reasons why they must purchase your product/service. Then, pushing further, your tag question elicits a 'yes' response to the advantages they will enjoy.

🔵 **brilliant** recap

- 'But' cancels everything before it and the listener believes the most important statement follows it.

▶

- When giving negative feedback or criticism, always adhere to the pattern: *bad news + but + good news.* This will leave a positive feeling in the subconscious mind of the listener, which is always a good thing.

- Use 'and' to either introduce a new subject or lead your prospect towards your goal, like this: *bad new + but + good news + and.*

- When countering objections, use the objection reversal technique: *Agreement + reason for objection + but + confirm desire + because + specific benefits + tag question + solution.*

- To elicit a 'yes' response, ask tag questions like: Won't you? Can't you?

- Nod your head two or three times while asking a tag question. This secret body language technique will elicit an audible or silent 'yes' within your subject.

- Listen acutely to what people are saying, be vigilant, stop them from talking themselves into their reality when it does not suit you and always reverse a negative statement that uses the word 'but'.

CHAPTER 5

Rapport

Instantly establish resonant rapport

'You can close more business in two months by becoming interested in other people than you can in two years by trying to get people interested in you.'

Dale Carnegie

apport must exist between you and your subject for language patterns to work efficiently. No matter how expertly you have memorised and assimilated the persuasive techniques you have learnt into everyday conversations, there is little chance any will produce the results you seek if you have not developed a significant degree of rapport.

In this chapter, we examine a few of the more established techniques for developing a connection with others, which you, more than likely, are already using, then we progress towards a more unconventional and somewhat covert method used by highly experienced persuaders. First, though, let us determine what rapport is exactly because, when we know this, we will be best placed to recognise easily when we have successfully created it!

Definitions of rapport

- A close and balanced relationship in which the people or groups concerned understand each other's feelings or ideas and communicate well.
- A real appreciation of someone and an ability to converse naturally with them.
- A relationship of shared understanding or trust and agreement between two people.

Few, we suspect, would disagree with these definitions. Appreciating what has to occur to create rapport, perhaps it is easy to understand how it can take some of us quite some time to achieve.

When I first discovered the technique, I questioned whether it would work for me, and wanted to start practising immediately. Choosing a local supermarket, patiently waiting my turn to empty my trolley (and following the process that we will reveal later), I engaged the young woman about to check out my items in conversation. The result was amazing: from a relatively sullen expression, her face lit up; we chatted like old friends, to the considerable annoyance of those behind me in the queue.

Rapport and body language

Rapport is a characteristic of subliminal human interaction. Every day, we radiate our intentions, feelings and moods to others through our body language. Those around us respond to us at this unconscious level. To establish rapport, we must take the initiative and actively create otherwise subliminal messages and direct them to the area of least resistance in others, their subconscious mind. Eventually, these messages will reveal themselves as conscious ideas, actions, beliefs, moods and, most importantly, acceptance.

Why we develop rapport:
- To ensure your prospect feels at ease in your presence.
- To successfully deliver persuasive language patterns.
- To be liked.
- To lead and direct your business conversations.
- To achieve your goals.
- To remove resistance and raise responsiveness.

Content-based rapport

First, we are going to mention a little about content-based rapport; it is an excellent technique that works well to break the ice, assuming you are in your prospect's personal office. If they are sharing a colleague's office, it will not work for reasons that will become apparent.

In the early 1980s, I was an aspiring recruitment consultant, engaged in research with a brief to identify potential candidates for assignments awarded to our consultancy. Always keen to progress my career, I vigilantly reviewed the situations vacant adverts in the national press. On one occasion, I spotted an advertisement for a senior researcher for one of London's most prestigious executive search consultancies. Shortly after sending my curriculum vitae, I was invited to attend an interview with the managing director of their telecommunications division.

The meeting was somewhat challenging. Seated in an uncomfortable chair rather too near to the ground, I peered nervously upwards at a charismatic and confident individual who, oddly, hardly spoke. Lacking confidence and wanting to leave, somewhat desperately I scanned the office and, spotting a motorcycle helmet, began questioning my interviewer about motorcycles and rallies.

From that point, the conversational dynamic was transformed. He talked with such enthusiasm about his hobby and I was feeling slightly less tense. Regretfully, a second interview did not materialise. This is an example of content-based rapport.

The aim of this approach is to discover what interests your prospect and to absorb as much information as possible about them from their office and allow them to talk freely on their favourite subjects. When you are listening, you must show genuine and sincere interest; fake it and you will fail. By doing this, a bond is formed; you have, likely, shared comparable experiences, your prospect will consider you similar to them, and people like doing business with people like themselves.

The reason for this is incredibly simple: most of us think of ourselves as being 'pretty much okay' and, without giving this much thought, we use this internal perception of ourselves as a gauge for how we view others and, therefore, anyone like us, in some way, is clearly someone with whom we will work happily.

If your prospect is in someone else's office, or if you have detected they are a private individual uncomfortable talking about their hobbies or family, process-based rapport development is likely to be the most useful option.

Process-based rapport

If you sense your prospect is somewhat reticent about discussing personal issues, or their office is void of personal effects, it is best to direct the conversation towards their work environment. You may share similar corporate experiences, be located in the same vicinity, have similar company structures, and so on.

The same rules apply to process-based as to content-based rapport; you must express genuine interest and be sincere at all times. As you share collective experiences and appear similar, a connection will develop.

Content-based and process-based rapport development are two of the millions of results currently popping up if you search the internet for, 'how to develop rapport'. They are equally well documented and taught at length in most traditional sales training seminars. Other techniques include:

- mirroring and matching body language;
- copying the way your prospect speaks;
- breathing in and out as your prospect breathes in and out;

- talking at the same speed as your prospect;
- repeating and approving what your prospect says.

These are all excellent methods, but imagine having to remember to use them all, to know when to use them, to be relaxed during your presentation and to be persuasive and promote your products or services. With so much happening, it is not surprising that most people give up because, in reality, juggling these techniques can be distracting and diverts your energy away from delivering a relaxed, informative presentation.

As Brilliant Persuaders, you will learn how to develop rapport instantly, with a subtle and incredibly powerful single technique, an approach not ordinarily covered in traditional inhouse or external sales training events that relies, as we mentioned initially in this chapter, on the *proactive* transference of subliminal messages.

brilliant tip

If you currently use an effective method of building rapport, retain it in your arsenal of techniques and add this instant rapport-building technique to enhance the effectiveness of your encounters with others.

How to develop instant rapport

First, let me say I have applied this approach for many years and regularly taught it to my teams. Whatever your area of business, this technique produces results. This simple and straightforward four-step procedure requires a small measure of mental gymnastics and has to be one of the best ways of quickly developing rapport with those you are meeting for the first time.

Step 1   You would agree that most people can visualise, wouldn't you? For a moment, I would like you, in your mind's eye, to picture yourself walking into a room and greeting a close friend. (I do not mean a very, very close friend.) Perhaps someone from school or university, maybe the mechanic in the garage you have been taking your car to for years. Alternatively, maybe a current client with whom you feel particularly at ease. Make the image of the encounter vibrant, larger than life and as realistic as you can.

Step 2   Notice in your mind's eye what is different about your body language. How are you standing, walking as you encounter those with whom you have already established rapport compared to how you might look meeting someone for the first time? Primarily, you are more relaxed and exuding confidence; you have an aura of friendliness, of cordiality towards and acceptance of the other party, and this is revealed in your demeanour. Continue to imagine the encounter.

Step 3   Now, as you continue seeing yourself, bring to the surface the feelings and emotions you are experiencing. Capture those feelings, re-experience them intensely. You are calm, at ease, happy, confident and relaxed. Continue experiencing these emotions as you see yourself in your mind's eye.

Step 4   Bring together the image of yourself and the feelings you are experiencing and, when they are at their peak, at the same time, squeeze

your thumb and first finger of either or both
hands and associate the physical action with
the feelings you are experiencing and the
images you have seen.

That's it!

Next time you meet a new prospect, take a few moments, squeeze
together your thumb and first finger and allow the images and
feelings of meeting an existing contact flood your mind, then
proceed with your meeting.

When you have mastered the skill of meeting new people for the
first time like this, you are conveying to their subconscious mind
powerful subliminal signals, messages to which they have no
choice but to respond instinctively. You have chosen to take control of the meeting from the outset.

---

brilliant action

Actively observe how others will start to relate to you more positively as you
proactively induce rapport. Hone your skills; this is incredibly powerful.

I always remember a particular occasion when I decided to use
the instant rapport-building technique. In my late twenties, I was
meeting, for the first time, on a one-on-one basis, the chairman
and chief executive of a global data telecommunications company at his private club. I practised the technique before the
meeting and, to this day, recall it as one of the most satisfying
and financially rewarding presentations I have ever delivered.
Anxiety evaporated as apparent old friends discussed the project
at hand.

![brilliant] action

Practise building instant rapport with everyone you encounter, from the post person you might see every morning, the garage attendant, the person who checks out your groceries at the supermarket, at the off-licence, and your local 24/7 store. As your confidence increases, introduce the technique with prospects and clients.

![brilliant] recap

The secret method to induce and develop a deep rapport with someone you have not met is to create within yourself a mental attitude that you already have it. It is that simple! Greet new people as if they are family members or close friends. By doing this, you will naturally exude subliminal messages of warmth, confidence and acceptance, and those around you will instinctively feel the same and reciprocate.

CHAPTER 6

Because logic

Intensify your powers of influence, instantly!

'Influence is our inner ability to lift people up to our perspective.'

Joseph Wong

I n this chapter, you discover how, by deliberately deciding to use the word 'because' strategically in conversations, you will raise your level of influence and boost your powers of persuasion. Sales conversations will flow naturally and your prospects will be more responsive to your suggestions.

From childhood, the word 'because' is embedded in our young minds, from having asked questions such as:

- 'Why must I go to bed now?'
- 'Why have I got to eat this?'

The answers we would, invariably, receive were, respectfully, 'Because I say so' and 'Because it is good for . . .' I am sure you remember replies like these and, maybe if you have young children, you are responding similarly to them. Notice how the answers to these questions begin with the word 'because'.

As youngsters, our parents, as theirs with them, unwittingly programmed us to believe and accept whatever followed the word 'because' to be an appropriate, truthful answer to any question we raised beginning with the word 'why'. Of course, we probably did not realise this at that time. As Brilliant Persuaders, we revisit this phenomenon and use it to our advantage.

Dr Ellen Langdon, a Psychology Professor at Harvard University, conducted a three-part scientific experiment that rocked the world of persuasion, with students standing in line at a photocopying machine. We have outlined the basics here:

- *Stage 1:* A student was directed to the head of the queue to ask the next person in line to use the copier, 'Excuse me, can I go in front of you?' With no reason to jump in given, almost 60 per cent moved to one side and allowed this person to jump the queue.

- *Stage 2:* On the next occasion, the student was asked to proceed to the front of the line and say to the person at the head of the queue, 'Excuse me, can I go ahead of you *because* I am in a hurry?' Amazingly, almost 94 per cent of the time, they were allowed to jump the queue. The reason 'being in a hurry' appeared to be appropriate enough for others to comply with the request.

- *Stage 3:* In the last stage of the experiment, the student was asked to approach the front of the line and say, 'Excuse me, may I go ahead of you *because* I need to make some copies?' Not a viable reason at all, except the word 'because' was used. Astonishingly, the compliance rate remained almost the same as stage 2 of the experiment, at 93 per cent, just by using the word 'because'.

Summary:

Stage	Because logic	Reason	% compliance
Stage 1	Not used	None given	60%
Stage 2	Used	Given	94%
Stage 3	Used	None given	93%

Because the findings collected from Langdon's research experiment were so conclusive, they proved, in the field of persuasion, the irrefutable importance and influence of the word 'because'.

The 'because response' conditioning we received as children remains within us in adulthood and is exceptionally relevant today, particularly when we respond to questions posed by our prospects. Remember, they were programmed in an identical manner by their parents.

Essentially, because of early indoctrination, resistance is reduced and information is believed and more likely to be unhesitatingly acceded to by others when it is preceded by the word 'because'.

brilliant tip

Remember, we were all programmed during our childhood to respond in the same way to the word 'because'. Because most people give this little thought, as Brilliant Persuaders, start purposefully capitalising on the effect this word has on others with your friends and colleagues before progressing to important business presentations.

Why we use because logic to answer questions

- Because we know that everything we say will be accepted more readily.

- Because we can provide more information than is being requested, and would choose to do this when it is evident our prospect would be positively influenced by the answers to questions they had not asked.

- Because it is an excellent opportunity to plant suggestions and guide the subject of any conversation towards our objective.

In the following examples, each question is answered twice; the first reply is typical of how most would respond. The second reply, because it incorporates 'because logic', is naturally more persuasive, plants suggestions and permits the respondent to exercise greater control over the conversation.

Prospect	What does your product/service offer us that we are not already happily receiving from XYZ?

Response 1	I know XYZ. They have an excellent portfolio; our equivelent unit has increased flexibility and it is more efficient in terms of running costs.
Response 2	I know XYZ. They have an excellent portfolio. Because we are the market leader in this sector, this mean that we have a larger R&D budget than any other company; our equivalent unit hit the market six months ago with fantastic reviews. It is more efficient and its running costs are lower.
Response analysis	The second response not only effectively answers the question, but also reinforces the status of the supplier as the market leader.
Prospect	What experience does your firm have in our industry?
Response 1	We have worked with many of the top IT recruiters over the past decade and have a proven track record.
Response 2	Because my own background is in the IT sector, I have a particular understanding of the type of issues that can crop up. Our company has a 10-year track record in the technology sector.
Response analysis	Not only is the question answered, the potential client has learnt they are dealing with an acknowledged IT specialist.
Prospect	Will this investment yield what you are quoting?
Response 1	Yes, absolutely. Let's review its history and projections further.

Response 2	Yes, because most people trust us with their life savings and pension funds. Let's examine the history and projections further.
Response analysis	The second response not only answers the question, it embeds into the conversation the important suggestion, 'most people trust us'.

brilliant action

Actively observe how others more readily accept the answers to their enquiries when they are preceded by the word 'because'.

brilliant tip

Because the word 'because' is recognised as powerfully persuasive, use it proactively whenever you can. It will extend your perceived level of influence and enable you to lead and direct conversations with ease.

brilliant recap

- Everything said after the word 'because' is pre-supposed to be true because it is!
- By adding 'because' to a request, you are guaranteed to increase your compliance rate.
- Using the word 'because' instantly heightens your level of influence.
- Use 'because' more often to answer questions.
- Practise by preparing lists of typical questions; write down and remember your replies.
- To build your confidence, use 'because logic' in a stress-free environment with your family, acquaintances and work colleagues.
- Answer every question beginning with 'why' with 'because'.

CHAPTER 7

Awareness patterns

Gain unconditionally acceptance of everything you say

'The first step towards change is awareness; the second is acceptance.'

Nathaniel Branden

I n this chapter, we introduce a group of words that will allow you to enjoy more influence over your prospects and make sure they jump to the conclusions you wish and think what you want them to think. You will discover ways to:

- bypass resistance;
- increase responsiveness;
- embed ideas and suggestions;
- effortlessly deliver powerful pre-suppositions and assumptions.

Awareness – what is it and what does it really mean? Does it mean anything other than just having knowledge? When sales professionals promote products and services to their prospects, face to face, via email or in a brochure, it is customary to inform and educate potential purchasers vis-à-vis the unique selling points of their particular product or service. Isn't it?

For example, let us consider the retail homeware sector. A shopper, considering the purchase of a set of pans, might ask, 'Why should I buy these? What's different about them?' The sales assistant could say something like:

- They have a special coating, unique to this manufacturer, which ensures nothing sticks to them.
- The high-quality manufacturing ensures they will last longer than any others at this price point.

- They are manufactured in Germany.
- They come in a range of colours.

Now, the potential buyer is perfectly informed and has sufficient information to make an educated purchasing decision. Let us now consider a firm of accountants, promoting their professional services to a self-employed local business person. They may say:

- We'll undertake all your VAT administration. Provide us with your purchase and sales vouchers and we will administer everything else.
- We are local and, if you have immediate concerns, call us and we will send an account manager to your office immediately.
- Our company structure enables us to offer accounting services more quickly than any other firm.
- The majority of our clients are sole traders; we understand your needs.
- We have a team specialising in your industry.

Once again, the prospect has all the facts required to make a decision to either retain this firm or continue exploring the market.

As you consider these examples, you may have noticed the sales approach or part, at least, might be analogous to your own. You can see that the prospect receives a list of unique selling points. Most sales professionals realise the importance of providing appropriate information to guide their prospects towards making buying decisions

Does this approach border on a 'hard sell'? The benefits are conveyed to the customer and there is no attempt to bypass resistance or increase responsiveness, other than, maybe, initiating curiosity. Which is a good start? I realise, as you continue to read, doubtless you have in mind how you would approach this sales scenario and have methods in mind that work for you. How does the expression go? If it's not broken, don't fix it. So, I expect you are curious to learn how to enhance your approach. Our objective in this chapter is not to suggest you discard any sales method that periodically produces results, but to augment it. By increasing your awareness of the effect certain words have on others, so you can integrate them into your sales style and way of working.

What are awareness patterns?

When we say 'awareness patterns', we are referring to a small set of words in the English language that imply awareness or knowledge and, compellingly, everything said after them is pre-supposed to be true.

When you use these words to describe the benefits of any product or service, the *only* open question is your prospect's 'awareness' of the advantages of your offering.

Consider these examples:

---

brilliant examples

Example 1

Sales consultant	The special coating on these pans ensures that nothing will stick to them.
Response analysis	The customer will question, or have doubts about, the effectiveness of the coating and may think, 'I'm not so certain' or 'Really?'

Example 2

Sales consultant	You'll notice the unique surface coating on these pans prevents anything from sticking to them.

▶

Response analysis	The question is: has the customer noticed the coating? Crucially, the question is *not:* 'Does the coating work?' This statement bypasses resistance and increases responsiveness. The buyer is informed what the seller wants them to accept as true, which may elicit either a spoken or unspoken response, 'That sounds good' or 'I'd not noticed the coating. Let me see it.' The awareness pattern 'word' facilitating this reaction is 'notice'.

Example 3

Sales consultant	We have a team specialising in your industry.
Response analysis	The customer may think, 'Do you?' or 'Really? Specialising in *my* industry!'

Example 4

Sales consultant	Do you realise we have a team specialising in your industry?
Response analysis	The question asked of the potential client is do they 'realise' a specialist team exists? There is no doubt about the existence of the team, which is the USP. In this example, information is pre-supposed and unquestioned, responsiveness increased and resistance lowered. The 'awareness pattern' word facilitating this response is 'realise'.

I wonder if you noticed the awareness vocabulary in an earlier paragraph? For ease, here it is again; we have italicised the awareness pattern words:

As you consider these examples, you may have *noticed* the sales approach or part, at least, might be analogous to your own. You can *see* that the prospect receives a list of unique selling points. Most sales professionals *realise* the importance of providing appropriate information to guide their prospects towards making buying decisions.

Upon your first reading of this paragraph, it is unlikely you noticed the intentional use of awareness pattern words deliberately planted with the sole aim of gaining your acceptance of the messages contained in the paragraph. Can you recall how you felt as you read this? Did you question anything in the paragraph or agree with what was written?

Awareness pattern words include:

- notice;
- see;
- realise;
- aware;
- experience;
- discover.

brilliant tips

- Most people already unconsciously use the vocabulary of awareness. As Brilliant Persuaders, you should deliberately choose these words when it is necessary to intensify an individual's awareness or gain agreement about something that is important to you.

- Start describing your products and services actively using the vocabulary of awareness. Few will state they have not seen/ realised, are not aware or have not experienced or noticed anything you say.

To reinforce awareness pattern words, consider these questions:

● Are you *aware* most people often assume that whatever someone says after the word *notice* is correct and hardly ever questioned? *See!* You have *noticed* the assumption in this statement, haven't you? (Are you re-reading it?)

● Have you *noticed* most people never question what they are told when it comes after the word *see?* You can *see* the implications here, can't you?

● Are you *aware* that questions containing the word *realise* are usually taken to be the truth, without question? Do you *realise* how important this question is?

● Do you *realise* that people automatically take what is said following the word *aware* as fact? Don't they? I am *aware* you are *aware* this is true! Isn't it?

● You have probably *discovered* how easy it is to start to use awareness patterns every day to maximise your sales, haven't you?

↗ exercise 1

Below are examples of questions with awareness vocabulary. With your product/service in mind, complete each question by adding the knowledge you wish your prospect to accept subliminally without question. Use them in your next sales presentation.

● Have you noticed . . . ?

● Can you see . . . ?

● Have you realised . . . ?

● Have you already realised . . . ?

● Did you realise . . . ?

● Are you aware . . . ?

● Have you ever experienced . . . ?

As you review these, you will notice they all go against everything frequently explained about questioning technique because they are all closed questions. Remember, in this case, our primary objective is to plant suggestions containing pre-suppositions that we are inviting our prospect to accept as true; we are not seeking the answers to the questions.

As you become aware of the influence you will enjoy by using awareness patterns in your presentations, I invite you to notice how easy it is to plant suggestions into minds of your prospects and clients. Once you start to use awareness vocabulary like this, you will realise quickly that the days of the 'hard sell' are truly over!

---

brilliant action

Please take a moment and re-read the last paragraph and identify the pre-suppositional statements inherent within it. These contain the concepts we want you to accept without objection. This is an example of using awareness patterns to gain agreement. If you have not spotted them, review the analysis below:

● The phrase 'As you become *aware*' directs you towards the first pre-supposition; we want you to accept that awareness patterns will be powerfully effective in your sales presentations.

● The phrase 'I invite you to *notice*' politely directs you towards the second pre-supposition; we want you to accept how easy it is to plant suggestions into the minds of your prospects with awareness patterns.

● The phrase 'You will *realise* quickly' directs you towards accepting that the days of the 'hard sell' truly are over.

You will notice it is the ideas that follow the awareness words that we want you to believe. Even if you are not aware, have not noticed or realised anything, you have heard the suggestions and our mission is achieved.

Now you can see how efficiently awareness patterns will enable you to guide your prospects to think about precisely what you want them to think! (Just keep using them!)

brilliant recap

- The vocabulary of awareness includes the words: notice, see, realise, aware, experience and discover.

- Everything you say following an awareness word will be pre-supposed to be true.

- Most people will not question assumptions made like this because, by hearing the statement, they will believe they ought to be aware or have realised, noticed or experienced whatever it is you are suggesting.

- This language pattern directs your prospect's attention towards the awareness word, ensuring everything following it is accepted as fact.

- Use the vocabulary of awareness to embed ideas and suggestions, bypass resistance, increase responsiveness and deliver powerful pre-suppositions.

- If anyone considers themselves unaware of anything you have said, they are unlikely to say so, and it doesn't matter because you have already successfully planted in their minds exactly what you want them to think.

CHAPTER 8

Verbal pacing and leading

Rapidly bypass criticism and gain agreement

'Influence is the compass; persuasion is the map.'

Joseph Wong

What is pacing and leading?

Verbal pacing and leading is a simple, yet powerful, conversational language pattern that allows you to quickly gain agreement for your suggestions and ideas, bypass criticism and increase your level of influence. This is an outstanding technique for eliciting positive responses and lowering your prospect's resistance. Curiously, it is not perceptible to the listener, it takes a little preparation and is an excellent tactic for increasing sales.

The process we follow when engaging with others is to make four statements. The initial three, referred to as *pacing statements,* are designed to be accepted without resistance and often without comment. The fourth *leading statement* is the suggestion for which we want unconditional acceptance.

As you continue reading and learning more about this technique, you are going to discover what makes verbal pacing and leading so compelling. When you think about it, language is universal. It cannot be avoided. Because of your newly acquired skills, you should be able to persuade anyone in any situation; it would be good to be able to do that, wouldn't it?

As you study this technique, soon only a few might be able to escape your impressive persuasive skills. You could, naturally, persuade more prospects and clients and win more business than you ever thought possible. Before revealing the structure of the pattern enabling you to accomplish all of the above, let us examine the terms 'pacing' and 'leading' and clarify their meaning.

Pacing statements

When pacing someone, your conversation must be focused around obviously true, experientially verifiable situations or topics on which you both agree. We refer to these as 'truisms'. When you make these statements, the listener is likely to be thinking, 'Yes, that's right', 'yes' and 'yes' again. If you are familiar with creating 'yes sets', then I am sure you will agree this is a sophisticated form of that technique.

The listener does not even have to answer out loud as a non-verbal confirmation of the statements is all that is required. You will recognise the following examples as truisms.

These statements are obviously true:

● You have read the first four paragraphs of this chapter.

● You are learning about verbal pacing and leading.

● You have just read about truisms.

We use truisms because they:

● create a state of receptiveness in others;

● deepen rapport, remove resistance and raise responsiveness by establishing a series of 'yes sets';

● lead conversations towards your outcome;

● covertly prepare your prospect to accept leading suggestions.

Truisms are essential for building 'response potential'. The more response potential we generate (and remember, your subject will be unaware this is happening), the more likely your leading suggestions will be accepted without resistance.

Leading statements

Having created 'response potential' by progressively pacing truisms, we continue by making a 'leading statement'. This is the suggestion that you want your prospect to accept or think about your company, product or service.

There are two schools of thought concerning the most efficient words to ensure your prospect accepts your suggestions. Some believe people more readily accept suggestions when they imply there is a *chance* that what is being said will occur and use vocabulary such as, should, may, could and might. Others prefer to suggest *certainty* with words and phrases like, it is going to happen/ take place, must and will.

---

brilliant example

Leading statement	Because of your newly acquired skills, you *should* be able to persuade anyone in any situation.
Or	
Leading statement	Because of your newly acquired skills, you *will* be able to persuade anyone in any situation.

---

brilliant tip

As you start to create pacing and leading statements following the format outlined below, try switching between possibility and certainty. Carefully monitor the outcome and use whichever produces the best result for you.

Pacing and leading pattern structure

The structure of pacing and leading is surprisingly straightforward; we recommend preparing three pacing statements and one leading statement:

Pacing statement 1	As you continue reading . . .
Pacing statement 2	. . . and learning more about this technique . . .
Pacing statement 3	. . . you are going to discover what makes . . .
Leading statement 1	. . . verbal pacing and leading so compelling.
Analysis	You must agree with the initial three pacing statements, which purposefully lead the conversation towards the suggestion we want you to accept that verbal pacing and leading is compelling.

brilliant tips

- Before delivering your sales presentation, prepare in advance and memorise your pacing and leading statements.

- Repeating language patterns improves your chances of success.

Review the following example pacing and leading statements:

Pacing statement 1	When you think about it, language is universal.
Pacing statement 2	It cannot be avoided.
Leading statement 1	Because of your newly acquired skills, you should be able to persuade anyone in any situation. . .
Gain acceptance	. . . it would be good to be able to do that, wouldn't it?
Response analysis	You will notice we have started to increase the momentum by using only two pacing

statements, moving quickly towards a more powerful leading statement, suggesting that the acquisition of persuasion skills will enable you to persuade most people in most situations. To gain acceptance following the leading statement, we ask a question. A little question like this is called a 'tag question'; others include: Can't you? Won't you? Isn't it? Can't it? Doesn't it? And so on.

brilliant tip

To further encourage your prospect to agree with what you are saying, nod your head up to three times as you ask a tag question. Nodding, like yawning, is contagious. Try it.

Repetition of all language patterns is essential. Finally, we might say:

Pacing statement 1	As you study this technique . . .
Leading statement 1	. . . soon only a few might be able to escape your impressive persuasive skills.
Leading statement 2	You could, naturally, persuade more prospects and clients . . .
Close	. . . and win more business than you ever thought possible.
Response analysis	We raised the momentum even further with a single pacing statement, directing the conversation towards two leading statements, representing two key ideas we want you to accept. We close with the primary belief we want you to agree to, that mastering pacing and leading will

enable you to win more business than you ever thought possible.

The three sets of pacing and leading statements we have just reviewed are, of course, the third and fourth paragraphs of this chapter and follow this overall pattern:

Step 1	Step 2	Step 3
Pacing statement	Pacing statement	Pacing statement
Pacing statement	Pacing statement	Leading statement
Pacing statement	Leading statement	Leading statement
Leading statement	Gain acceptance	Close

The above combination of pacing and leading phrases builds momentum in your subject. We hoped, as you read the third and fourth paragraphs of this chapter, that you became enthused about the technique you were about to learn, a method of persuasion that promised you would be able to persuade in any situation with any person. If you were, the pattern achieved its purpose and we speculated as you continued: you were unaware the paragraphs you were reading followed a precise, pre-determined structure, subtly and progressively leading you towards a conclusion we wished you to accept.

brilliant tips

To establish a strategy for practising pacing and leading, first write down the objective or outcome you desire for a particular meeting. Then, prepare three statements, interspersing facts and suggestions about the company, product or service you want to relay to your prospect, using the format that follows. Remember, facts are pacing statements and suggestions are leading statements.

- Three facts followed by one suggestion.

- Two facts followed by one suggestion.

- One fact followed by two suggestions.

- Close.

Practise saying your statements and suggestions out loud. The more you practise, the more it will naturally flow.

brilliant recap

- The pacing and leading pattern must begin with obvious factual statements (truisms) and progress to suggestions and/or questions.

- Always have a clear outcome in mind.

- Plan your pacing and leading statements, make a list of facts, advantages and benefits that your prospect can expect to enjoy when they purchase your product/service.

- Create a list of truisms, 'Thanks for inviting me here today' and 'Today we are going to introduce/talk about XYZ.' These two are easy to remember and will get you started.

- Leading statements describe what you want your prospect to think about your product, service or company. They can also be questions.

- Experiment by creating two sets of leading statements; one suggesting certainty and the other implying the possibility that what is being said will happen. Use whichever works best for you.

▶

- Build your confidence, practise saying your pacing and leading statement out loud in a non-pressurised environment.

- Start small with a single-stage statement, for example: 'Pace-pace-lead'. Once you see how easy it is to assimilate this into a conversation, and you notice how well it will be received, your confidence will increase, and you can introduce more stages.

- Keep everything simple.

- When both parties agree that a statement is irrefutably true, it is a truism.

- While pacing, watch out for nods from your subject; this is an indication that they are in agreement with you. Nods are instinctive 'tells' and valuable 'frame of mind' indicators.

- Pacing and leading works incredibly well in written form. Start incorporating the pattern into sales letters, emails and texts.

Once you master verbal pacing and leading, you will find it easy to influence almost anyone you need to. Practise and enjoy this powerful technique.

CHAPTER 9

Feel felt found

Magically resolve every objection with empathy and understanding

'The secret of man's success resides in his insight into the moods of people and his tact in dealing with them.'

J.G. Holland

I n this chapter, we present a covert language pattern for overcoming objections called 'feel felt found'. It is a useful technique that can be sneaked almost imperceptibly into conversation and is especially effective should your customer offer a quick off-the-cuff negative reaction to your product or service. We:

- illustrate the structure of this pattern and describe how you can interweave it seamlessly into your sales conversations;
- analyse what makes it so efficient;
- show how you can make it even more effective.

The structure of the pattern

This technique has three steps and, as its name implies, each step uses one of the following words: feel, felt or found. Once you have heard an objection or your client/prospect expresses a view counter to your goal, starting with step 1 you would say:

- I appreciate how you might *feel* about ABC.
- Most people have *felt* the same way.
- Everyone *found* . . . once they had bought/tried.

Elaborating a little more, let us have a look at each phrase in turn.

Step 1   I appreciate how you might *feel* about ABC.

Saying you recognise, and are aware of, how others might *feel* about something displays empathy and reveals you are compassionate towards their point of view. You will begin to establish an emotional connection with your prospect, which helps to bypass any criticism and raises responsiveness to your message. It is vital to be genuine when indicating an appreciation of your prospect's stance. If you fake this, you will fail.

Step 2   In step 2 you candidly reveal that: most people have *felt* the same way.

You might have heard of the expression 'misery seeks company'. In this expression, it is implicit that fellow sufferers make discontentment easier to tolerate. Of course, we are not implying your client is miserable. However, when you say to a prospect, 'Others have *felt* the same as you', before going ahead with a purchase, immediately they are comforted and have confidence in the knowledge they are not alone and others like them have purchased the same product or service and, importantly, felt the same way.

Step 3   In step 3 we go one final stage closer towards removing resistance and escalating their comfort level by saying: everyone *found,* once they purchased XYZ, the resultant advantages and benefits far exceeded their initial expectations.

This statement gently guides your prospects to take part in the discovery of the solution by informing them, when others looked closer, that they discovered everything was fine. This supports your prospect's purchasing decision and they feel confident to proceed.

brilliant tip

It is vital to remember that the success of this technique pivots on the degree of sincerity and empathy you relay to your prospect. You *must* be believable and truly understand their situation.

brilliant example

A sales professional is promoting accounting software to a reticent prospect.

Prospect   What you've stated, on the face of it, looks like it might have potential, but it is so much more complicated than what we are used to.

Persuader   I appreciate why you might *feel* this way but, honestly, you are not alone. In our experience, many people, running a finance department of this size, *felt* the same as you do now. What's more, and this is the crucial point, once the software was fully integrated, everyone *found* the overall efficiency of the department went through the roof!

In this example, the prospect's assessment that the product is too complicated is perfect for the feel felt found treatment, as the conversation is redirected effortlessly towards emphasising the advantages of greatest interest to the potential purchaser.

brilliant action

Listen to yourself as you enunciate the separate phrases of this technique. Practise acquiring an empathetic tone of voice. For example, should you say to a prospect, 'I can appreciate how you might feel that way' in a clipped staccato manner, their internal voice immediately informs them, 'Oh, no, you don't,' creating resistance and defeating the object of the pattern.

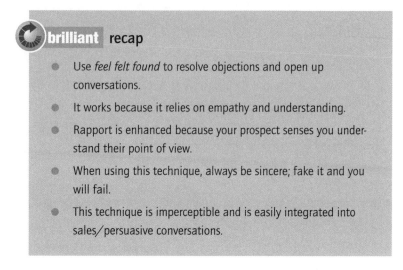

brilliant recap

- Use *feel felt found* to resolve objections and open up conversations.
- It works because it relies on empathy and understanding.
- Rapport is enhanced because your prospect senses you understand their point of view.
- When using this technique, always be sincere; fake it and you will fail.
- This technique is imperceptible and is easily integrated into sales/persuasive conversations.

CHAPTER 10

Internal representations

Secretly direct others to think what you want them to think

'Imagination is the beginning of creation. You imagine what you desire; you will what you imagine and, at last, you create what you will.'

George Bernard Shaw

What are internal representations?

Internal representation is the term we use to describe how we internally represent and attribute meaning to the outside world.

How do we use internal representation to persuade?

A uniquely effective method to persuade someone to your point of view or, to put this more strongly, communicate to others precisely what we want them to think, is to initiate within them a journey of thought and imagination to directly and proactively influence their internal representations in line with your objectives. If you suggest to someone to imagine something, whatever they see in their mind's eye they will believe is their idea, because they have generated it and brought it into conscious thought.

Imagine you are selling products or services. By using language in a particular way, you can actively lead your prospect to exercise their imagination. We do this using a combination of precisely describing what you want others to imagine and ultimately believe and, by asking specific questions designed to trigger their imagination, this will enable you to:

● shape your customer's internal representations (how they 'uniquely' perceive your product/service and associated advantages of ownership);

- persuade them more effectively;
- overcome objections and criticism.

Now, take a little more time than usual as you read this paragraph slowly and think about what it will mean to you when you acquire the skill to direct and lead the imagination of others proactively and positively towards the benefits of your product or service. Imagine what having that skill would be like and then think through all of the advantages you will enjoy. It is possible, isn't it, even to contemplate financial independence?

What if you could easily initiate desire in others for your products, services or ideas? Imagine how much more successful you will be and what this success would mean to you and your family.

Before we look into how to proactively initiate internal representations in the minds of others, let us think through what happens in your prospect's mind when you are in conversation with them or delivering a presentation.

You would be surprised at how much information your prospects receive consciously and subconsciously. For starters, they hear and see you and form an opinion about you instantly, based on their perception, which, in turn, is linked to the subliminal signals you reveal and their accumulated experience of interpreting such information, right or wrong! There is a lot to take in. To make sense of it all, their brain filters this information, it deletes some, distorts and generalises the rest. To understand the meaning of your presentation, they create unique mental images of the filtered information, these are the 'internal representations' you will learn to control and direct in this chapter.

The internal representations fuse with your prospect's emotions and create new ones at the time of your presentation; they may be happy, sad or even confused. And this, in turn, merges with what they are doing, sitting, standing or moving around – we call that their physiology. Eventually, your prospect understands and takes meaning from what you are saying.

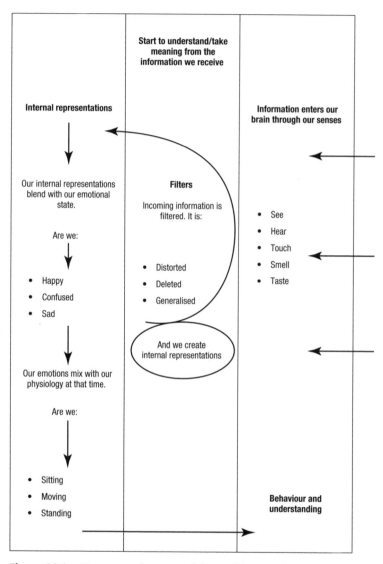

Figure 10.1   How we make sense of the world around us

One of our objectives as persuaders is to trigger the imagination of others to create intense internal representations of our ideas, our products and the actions we want others to take, in a way that it is important to them.

brilliant tip

When you start to use the vocabulary of internal representation, your prospects sell themselves on the advantages of your product or service because you have spurred their imagination. They see in their mind's eye how your offering brings benefits.

At this stage, I would like you to re-read an earlier paragraph of this chapter. Here it is again:

> Now, take a little more time than usual as you read this paragraph slowly and think about what it will mean to you when you acquire the skill to direct and lead the imagination of others proactively and positively towards the benefits of your product/service. Imagine what having that skill would feel like and then think through the benefits you will enjoy. It is possible, isn't it, even to contemplate financial independence?

When you read this for the first time, did you:

- *think about* what it will mean to you when you acquire the skill to direct and lead the imagination of others proactively and positively towards the benefits of your product/service?
- *imagine* what having that skill would feel like?
- *think through* the benefits you will enjoy?
- *contemplate* financial independence?

When we use the following words, we proactively compel our prospects to begin a mental journey of imagination that we have initiated, whether they are listening to us or reading our proposal documentation, and whatever they imagine is unique to them:

- Consider/considered
- Contemplate for a moment
- Think about/through
- What if
- What's it like when
- Imagine/imagined
- How about
- If you could have
- What would/will it be like if/when
- Suppose
- Think through
- Ponder
- Mull over
- Reflect on

brilliant action

Everyone uses the vocabulary of internal representation without knowing they are doing so and have no idea of the high level of influence it has on others, both consciously and subconsciously. Now you are aware of the powers wielded upon the imaginations of others by using these words, imagine the increased levels of success you will experience by actively integrating them into your speech, emails and text messages.

In each of the following examples, the client is directed to think about and imagine exactly what the sales professional wants them to think.

brilliant examples

Accounting software sales

- Just for a moment, *think through* the benefits an accounting system like this will bring to you and this company.
- *Consider* the range of advantages this accounting system has over others at the same price point.
- *What if* this software paid for itself in the first six months?

Retail sales

- *Think about* how confident you will feel when you wear this suit to your next presentation/interview.
- Can you *imagine* that extra touch of sophistication this lighting will bring to your home?
- *What if* I could offer you a deal on this dining service?

Double glazing sales

- *What if* your utility bills were 60 per cent less after you double glaze your entire house?
- *Imagine* your family being much more secure in your home.
- *Suppose* the savings you will make fitting this double glazing meant it would pay for itself in under two years.

Financial services

- *Imagine* all the things you will be able to do, if you could retire early.
- *What would it be like* when you have a tax-free lump sum of £500,000 for anything you want?
- *Think about* the implications of not having a plan like this in place.

Property sales

- Just *imagine* yourself living in an apartment like this.
- *If you could have* a place like this to bring up a family, wouldn't it be amazing?

● *What would it be* like entertaining all your friends in a dining room like this?

Telecommunication sales

● *How about* comparing your current mobile phone to the latest iPhone?

● *What if you could have* any telephone in this shop; which one would you choose?

Persuasion sales

● *What would it mean to you* if you could have the ability to generate more new business?

● *What if* you were financially independent within the next five years?

● Imagine how you would spend all the extra money you would make after you learn the persuasive techniques revealed in the Proactive Persuasion Seminar.

brilliant recap

● Proactively use the vocabulary of internal representations to enable others to begin an imaginary journey that you control regarding your products/services and the actions you want them to take.

● When you talk or write to your clients, use the vocabulary of internal representation to compel them to create mental images in their minds to understand and make sense of your messages.

● The vocabulary of internal representations is present naturally in everyday conversation and becomes power packed only when proactively used with a goal in mind.

CHAPTER 11

Motivational direction

Discover the hidden driving force compelling your prospect to make purchasing decisions

'If you talk to a man in a language he understands, that goes to his head. If you talk to him in his language, it goes to his heart.'

Nelson Mandela

No doubt you have often heard others say, or maybe at some point you have said, 'He/she just isn't talking my language'. Imagine the negative implications of a prospect or client thinking this following or during an important meeting with you. Not a pleasant thought, is it? Reflect on those occasions when you believe you have made a brilliant presentation and were not awarded the project or sold your product. What if, no matter how excellently you presented your product/service, your language let you down?

Most sales professionals are entirely unaware of the conscious and unconscious significance of the words they use and the impact, directly and indirectly, they have on others. They blindly attempt to develop rapport in the way they always have because someone said, 'It always works for me.' Alternatively, they hold the belief warranted or otherwise they have a universally likeable personality. Then they proceed doggedly to present the unique selling points of their product or service and wonder why success, however defined, remains at worst elusive and at best inconsistent. Sound familiar?

Deepening rapport

In this chapter, we explore a covert and subtly powerful technique unfamiliar to most business development professionals designed to enable you to match a particular aspect of the language used by your prospects. The power of this simple technique lies in the fact that your prospect is completely unaware of what they reveal in their vocabulary and, most significantly, they will be oblivious to how you have chosen to tailor your language to match theirs which, in turn, deepens rapport, removes resistance and raises responsiveness.

Have you ever thought about what motivates you? Do you know why you choose one action over another? We are all driven by different influencing factors, so you would imagine there are thousands of different reasons why we choose certain paths over others, wouldn't you? Fundamentally, issues influencing our day-to-day decisions and those of our prospects can be divided into two groups. To varying degrees, we are all motivated, either:

- *towards* an objective; or
- *away* from a problem to reach a goal.

Recognising and responding accordingly to your prospects' motivational linguistic direction positions you ahead of the competition as regards your ability to persuade. Interacting with other using their linguistic style, bearing in mind they will be unaware of it, ensures you will secure their full attention.

This artful and subtle technique will deepen rapport, remove resistance and seamlessly place you on the same wavelength as your prospect.

Your goal

Whether motivated *towards* a goal or *away from* a problem, when talking about areas of significant interest, each group represents themselves subtly differently. When communicating with your prospects, your objective is to identify their motivational direction.

Once you have identified the vocabulary set they are using, continue your presentation or conversation using their lexis. Curiously, your prospect will be oblivious as to their motivational linguistic preferences and, while this may sound rather technical, it is quite straightforward to identify.

How to identify your prospect's motivational direction

The simplest way to determine a person's motivational direction is to listen carefully to the words they use, following the word 'because'. To initiate a 'because' response, all you have to do is ask questions beginning with the word 'why'.

brilliant examples

- I wonder if you could clarify *why* have/did/would/should/will/must/ is it that/is . . . ?
- Earlier, you mentioned ABC; *why* have/did/would/should/will/must/ is it that/is . . . ?
- I see you might not be interested in doing XYZ but, *why* have/did/ would/should/will/must/is it that/is . . . ?

Have you noticed how we softened the question by using a short phrase before the word why? This is called an *opening phrase* or *opener* for short, also occasionally referred to as a *weasel phrase*. Short sentences like these are used, as in this case, to guide us towards a leading question; sometimes they are used to deflect attention and reduce resistance.

brilliant example

You wouldn't want to *stop using your existing supplier* until you are sure XYZ Ltd provides a superior service.

The above example uses the opener, 'You wouldn't want to', which softens what follows and acts as a resistance reducer, lulling the listener into a feeling of security. We could not say outright to a prospect, 'Stop using your existing supplier.' Instead, in this example, we are indirectly attacking the competition, effectively saying what we want by passing it. This technique is called *preterition*.

Another way of eliciting a because response is to ask a closed question. Closed questions begin with words like 'Do', 'Could', 'Would', 'Can', 'Are', and 'Will'. Your prospect may answer either 'Yes because . . . ' or 'No because . . . '.

Influencing language for those motivated *towards* an objective

Once you have asked a 'Why' question, listen for the italicised words below and you will know you are talking with a *towards*-oriented person.

- Because the company must *attain* preferred supplier status.
- Because I *have* to move the company towards . . .
- Because the department needs to *achieve* . . .
- Because we have to show we can *obtain* . . .
- Because I need to *get* . . .
- Because once XYZ is *included*, we can complete . . .
- Because when we *achieve* the first level, it *will enable us to* . . .
- Because the tremendous *benefits* are worth the small risk.
- Because the *advantages* of proceeding far outweigh . . .
- Because we will *accomplish* so much more.

This list is by no means exhaustive. Words in this category are aquisitional; the user needs to gain something to *win, secure, collect, reap* rewards to achieve their goal.

Body language of *towards*-oriented people

There are a couple of traits to look for to help confirm your linguistic observations. Towards-oriented people often reveal inclusive body language. They are comfortable communicating within their personal spatial zone between 0.5 m and 1.5 m and, as a guide, they nod their heads up and down more often than shaking them from left to right.

brilliant tip

You may find some people mixing the language from each group. Should you spot this, concentrate on identifying the predominant linguistic preference.

Influencing language – for those motivated *away from* a problem

Once you have asked a 'Why' question, listen for the italicised words below and you will recognise an away-oriented person.

- Because we must *avoid* missing our Q3 target.
- Because if I/they/we can *solve* this issue now, it will prevent possible downtime later.
- Because if we *prevent* this from happening now, later we'll not *have to deal with* . . .
- Because if we *eliminate* the excess, we'll save on . . .
- Because we'll *stop* haemorrhaging money and that makes sense to me.
- Because if we *get rid of* that department, our overhead costs will reduce.
- Because I *won't have to* waste time and money running that inhouse facility.

- Because *fixing* this now . . .
- Because *it is not perfect.*

This list is by no means exhaustive. Words in this category are preventative, as the user needs to stop something from happening, fix or get rid of something to achieve his/her goal. Other terms include: *remove, exclude, abolish* and *eradicate.*

Body language of away-oriented people

Interestingly, away-oriented people may exhibit a more exclusive style of body language; they are less comfortable talking with others in their personal zone between 0.5 m and 1.5 m. And, as a guide, they are head shakers more than nodders.

Away-oriented people might consider towards-oriented people to be naïve, perceiving a gung-ho attitude with little concern for the details. Conversely, towards-oriented individuals might describe their away-oriented counterparts as conservative and slightly staid, as they spend too much time dwelling on the detail, not seeing the bigger picture and afraid of taking risks. In a commercial environment, 40 per cent of people are towards-oriented and 40 per cent are away-oriented; 20 per cent are both towards and away.

Suppose a potential client said something like the following:

Prospect　Yes, I can see some of the advantages your products have over what we currently use, but I'll need convincing before I am positive they'll enable us to achieve our Q3 objectives.

Persuader　Everything in our portfolio ensures you will not have to worry about hitting your Q3 goals. Let me show you the best way I can to eliminate your concerns.

The above response ostensibly satisfies the prospect's doubts, as the persuader confirms their products are geared to ensure their client's success.

However, it is wrong; it is reflective of how most might respond and does not mirror the prospect's preferred motivational linguistic preference. The prospect's cue words are: *enable* and *achieve* and the sales professional replied with *worry* and *eliminate*. This is very subtle, very powerful and missed by most.

A better response might be:

> *Persuader* Everything you'll *get* in the system I've described *enables* you to *accomplish* your Q3 objective. Have I mentioned that our products *include* a 15-year guarantee and onsite service?

This response recognises the client's preferred motivational direction as towards-oriented, by using the words, *get, enable* and *accomplish*. The prospect feels comfortable on a subconscious level and, most importantly, will be more receptive.

brilliant recap

- Prospects are motivated towards an objective or away from a problem to achieve their goal.

- Towards and away communication styles have unique language.

- Towards language includes the words: *attain, have, achieve* and *obtain*.

- Away language includes the words: *avoid, prevent, stop* and *eliminate*.

- Towards-oriented people have inclusive body language and tend to nod their heads.

- Away-oriented people have exclusive body language and tend to be head shakers.

▶

- Conversing with your prospects in their linguistic motivational style deepens rapport, removes resistance and increases responsiveness to your message on a subconscious level.

- If you hear both towards and away language, try to identify the most dominant.

CHAPTER 12

Testing for the truth

Decipher the secret messages revealed in your prospect's eyes

'I don't know the rules of grammar. If you're trying to persuade people to do something, or buy something, it seems to me you should use their language.'

David Ogilvy

Have you ever watched courtroom TV? The judge vigorously insists, while questioning the defendant or accused, that they look directly into their eyes. What exactly do you think they hope to find? In this chapter, we reveal two very useful techniques.

1 You'll discover how to determine if your prospects are telling the truth by carefully observing the instinctive movement of their eyes when responding to questions.

2 To deepen rapport, remove resistance and increase responsiveness. We'll show how to determine if your prospects are (V) visual, (A) auditory, (K) kinesthetic or (D) digital thinkers. We will clarify what this means and establish how their preferred thinking style influences their vocabulary and how you must adjust yours to match theirs.

The truth or not the truth

Imagine the eye area is divided into three horizontal planes: upper, middle and lower.

The upper *visual* plane

Figure 12.1　Constructed images

Should your subject move their eyes upwards, to your left, when responding to a question, this is an indication that they are forming images in their mind's eye to answer your question. It is possible that their response will be untruthful because they have to create something from nothing in order to reply. When you detect this movement, consider it as a prompt to enquire further about their answer, before assuming it is untrue.

Should their eye movements be upwards, to your right, when answering, they are reflecting on an event that has taken place and their response is likely to be truthful. If you observe your prospect's eyes in the upper visual plane more than any other, it is fair to assume their preferred thinking style is visual. Remember, your subject is unlikely to know this. Visual thinkers make sense of the world with pictures, drawings, diagrams, presentations and displays. They form memories and make decisions based on what they observe.

Figure 12.2　Remembered images

You have, undoubtedly, heard the English idiom, 'A picture is worth a thousand words'. To visual thinkers, it really is! Moreover, interestingly, they also have a preferred vocabulary. The following list provides a general indication of visual vocabulary. You will see why as you review the words. Watch your prospect's eye movements and listen to them using words and phrases like these.

Example vocabulary employed by visual thinkers:

Appear	Appearance	Blind	Bright	Brilliant
Cloudy	Dark	Dim	Dull	Envision
Faded	Gaze	Glance	Glare	Glimpse
Illuminate	Image	Light	Look	Lustre
Notice	Observe	Panorama	Pattern	Perspective
Picture	Review	Reveal	Scan	Scene
See	Show	Sight	Spy	Study
View	Viewpoint	Visible	Watch	

Example phrases used by visual thinkers:

Please *look* at this

Please *focus* in on this space

Draw a conclusion

There's *light* at the end of the tunnel

Look at this from my *perspective*

Show me how

This will shed *light* on the situation

Can you *see* it

This will *illustrate* my idea

Let's *map* out a plan

We'll have to *look* into this

The *vision* is clear

Picture this scenario

Just *scan* this for any issues

Selling to visual thinkers

Those showing a visual preference appreciate seeing pictures of concepts and ideas. If you have brochures, distribute them. If you can, draw your ideas. They will appreciate a 'Let me *show* you how this will work for you' approach more than others and welcome the use of white boards, flip charts, overhead projectors and PowerPoint presentations.

The mid *auditory* plane

Figure 12.3 Constructed sounds   **Figure 12.4** Remembered sounds

If a person's eyes move to their left or right, as if they are looking towards their ears, while answering a question, they are thinking auditorily about conversations and sounds they have had or have heard. If you ask an auditory thinker a question and he/she moves their eyes (in the mid plane) towards your left, they are constructing sounds and their answers will prompt further questioning, as they may be untrue. If their eyes move to your right, they are recalling actual sounds and conversations and their responses are likely to be truthful.

Regular eye movements in the mid-plane, more than any other, reveal a mostly auditory thinking style. Auditory thinkers make memories, decisions and sense of the world based on what they hear. They will remember names with ease and may struggle to recall faces; they might be less aware of what is going on around them visually; they like to talk on the phone rather than face to face and have a preferred vocabulary.

Examples of words used by auditory thinkers:

Aloud	Announce	Articulate	Call
Chat	Chime	Comment	Converse
Declare	Discuss	Express	Hear
Listen	Loud	Mention	Orchestrate
Quiet	Resound	Ring	Say
Sounds like	Speech	Talk	Tell
Told	Utter	Verbalise	Voice

Example phrases used by auditory thinkers:

I *hear* what you're saying	*Sounds* good to me
I *hear* you *loud* and clear	Please *voice* your opinion
That *rings* true to me	Gave me the *silent* treatment
We've got that *loud* and clear	Yes I am in *tune* with that
	Tune into your wavelength
Call me	Let's *chat* about the this
Sounds like you have sorted	central issues

Selling to auditory thinkers

Auditory thinkers like discussions and will appreciate a 'Let's *talk* through the main benefits and I'll send the paperwork later' approach. They are good listeners and enjoy precisely delivered presentations. If you know you are talking with an auditory thinker, vary your pitch and tone of your voice. They enjoy conversation more so than visual thinkers, so asking questions and initiating debate will work well.

> ### ☀ brilliant tip
>
> Be persistent and practise asking your friends and family simple questions while carefully monitoring their eyes. By doing this, you will reinforce your skills in a stress-free environment and the advantages you will acquire by using this information with your prospects and clients will bring tremendous results.

The lower kinesthetic plane

Figure 12.5   Kinesthetic

When people move their eyes downwards and to your left, they are thinking about a physical sensation or an internal feeling. We call this kinesthetic.

Examples of words used by kinesthetic thinkers:

Attach	Backing	Balance	Catch
Cold	Concrete	Cool	Cut
Exhale	Fear	Feel	Firm
Grab	Grasp	Hard	Link
Merge	Nervous	Point	Probe
Ragged	Rough	Sense	Solid
Stable	Steady	Stiff	Sturdy
Support	Tackle	Tender	Tension
Tight	Twist	Unbalanced	Uncomfortable
Weigh			

Example phrases used by kinesthetic thinkers:

We have to get a *feel* for

It is *irritating* to think that

We need *concrete* proof

We need a *solid* foundation

Can you *point* that out to me

Feel free to do as you wish about that

I am *not so comfortable*

Selling to kinesthetic thinkers

Kinesthetic thinkers appreciate the 'Let me walk you through this proposal and I will point out the key areas' approach. If you are selling a product that is portable, bring it to your meeting to be held, as kinesthetics are tactile – they like props and equipment and have a practical approach.

The lower digital plane

Figure 12.6   Auditory digital

When a right-handed subject looks down to your right, they are engaged an internal conversation, a dialogue with themselves. We call this digital (D) language; it is void of emotion. When this occurs, as further confirmation, watch if they slightly tilt their head to your right.

Once you have observed eye movement down to the right, you can, occasionally, encourage someone to say what he or she is thinking, by asking, 'What do you feel about this/that idea?' or 'What do you say to yourself when . . . ' They may respond with, 'I just thought that if . . . ' or, 'Oh, nothing. I was only . . . ' By asking these questions at the right time, your prospect may reveal information that helps guide your presentation in the right direction.

Digital thinkers are likely to use words that are void of emotion and have three or more syllables, such as:

Analyse	Benefit	Capability	Circumstance
Consider	Contemplate	Coordinate	Deliberate
Differentiate	Engage	Facilitate	Ingratiate
Initiate	Manifest	Motivate	Negotiate
Ponder	Pretend	Produce	Professional
Quality	Recognise	Remember	Respond
Results	Stabilise	Understand	Utilise
Wonder			

Example phrases used by digital thinkers:

We'll *deliberate* upon this theory.

I write concerning our recent *observation*.

We have *identified* the primary cause of the difficulty.

It is a matter of *professional* standards.

Selling to auditory digital thinkers

People in this group enjoy having the facts and thinking things through themselves. They appreciate handouts and perusing statistics and figures. They tend to be quite logical, so tailor your approach to appeal to this personality type. In general, they are less spontaneous than the other groups.

brilliant tip

Context and personal circumstances can affect a person's representational system. Regularly meeting your prospects and clients over time will offer an enhanced perception of their preferred linguistic preference.

Head movements and squinting

The combination of head and eye movements and squinting allows us tremendous insight regarding understanding what our prospects are thinking.

Squinting

If you ask a question and your prospect subtly squints their eyes, they are subconsciously trying to block that question and their response may be untruthful. This is called eye blocking. Squinting can also be seen while someone is reading something disagreeable. It will happen instantaneously without his or her awareness. This is a very useful 'tell' when negotiating contracts or devising plans.

Head movements

When a person responds to a question or statement and shakes their head either positively or negatively, *as they speak,* the likelihood is that they are being truthful. On the other hand, if the head movement occurs slightly *later than the speech,* there is a possibility they are being economical with the truth and, again, this is your prompt to investigate further.

Here are some examples of the correct and incorrect use of Visual, Auditory, Kinaesthetic and Digital (VAKD) language.

brilliant examples

Example 1

Prospect   Everything you've said so far *sounds* promising. I think you've *tuned* into the needs of our company.

You would *not* respond with:

Consultant   Yes, we thought about your corporate needs and I lead the team that *mapped* out this plan. We had a *vision* of what we thought would work best for you given the parameters you gave us.

The consultant has not *tuned* into the prospect's thinking style. The prospect clearly is an auditory thinker and the given response is visual. The adverse effects of the linguistic mismatch are subtle, as the prospect subconsciously ruminates upon the conversation. How much more appropriate is this response?

Consultant   Yes, we *heard* your requirements *loud* and clear and our team *tuned* into this plan, and we all thought it *rang true* with your requirements.

Example 2

Prospect   You need to show me *concrete* proof that what you're offering will satisfy our needs.

▶

You would *not* respond with:

> Consultant We've *identified* the main *requirements* and can assure you of the *effectiveness* of our product.

The prospect revealed a kinesthetic thinking style, while the consultant has responded digitally. The subtle mismatch will influence the level of rapport between customer and client and, possibly, even the choice of supplier. How much more aligned is this response?

> Consultant You can *relax* because we've researched your requirements in depth to the *point* we are 100 per cent confident you'll be delighted with what we have to offer.

Okay, I have deliberately exaggerated these examples to make the point, and:

● if you are a visual thinker, you will *see* where we are going with this;

● if you are an auditory thinker, everything you've just read *sounds* good;

● if you are a kinesthetic thinker, you've *grasped* the points we are making; and

● if you are a digital thinker, you've *differentiated* between the *alternative* thinking styles and can *appreciate* the benefits their use will bring.

As we reach the end of this chapter, the crucial message we wish to impart is to listen carefully for the language preferences unknowingly revealed by your prospects and clients. Always observe their eye movements as they speak and use this knowledge to reinforce your perception of their preferred linguistic style, then continue your presentation using their chosen vocabulary.

A cautionary note

Should you wish to determine if someone is economical with the truth, it is important to listen and look at the entire person.

Mastering this technique is challenging and will require practice. In general, when answering questions, should you observe others moving their eyes to your left in the mid and upper planes, further questioning may be required. However, there are some exceptions:

● We have established there are six directions in which the eyes can move, and each signifies a particular meaning. For some people, the direction in which he or she moves their eyes while being questioned is reversed (if they are left handed, for example). To determine if this is the case with your subject, observe their eyes while asking test questions, those to which you already know the answer. Now you can monitor the direction their eyes move when they are either constructing or remembering events as you have created a reference line for future questioning.

● We all process hundreds of thoughts simultaneously and, occasionally, when asking someone a question, many thoughts can rush into their minds and their eyes may move rapidly in any direction as each thought is processed and disregarded before an answer is given. Should this happen, it is impossible to detect if the answer is truthful or not.

● Some people focus and refocus their eyes when attempting to remember something and tend not to look in any particular direction. It is impossible to determine the truthfulness of any answer these people give.

● If your questions refer mainly to very recent events that remain in your subject's short-term memory, it is likely your prospect will look straight ahead while answering and, again, it will be impossible to verify the veracity of the response.

Things to look out for

To help establish if someone is left or right handed, when entering your prospect's office, observe the position of pens and the telephone on his/her desk. You could, reasonably, expect a right-handed person to place these items on their right; it is not set in stone, but many right-handed people wear their watch on their left wrist.

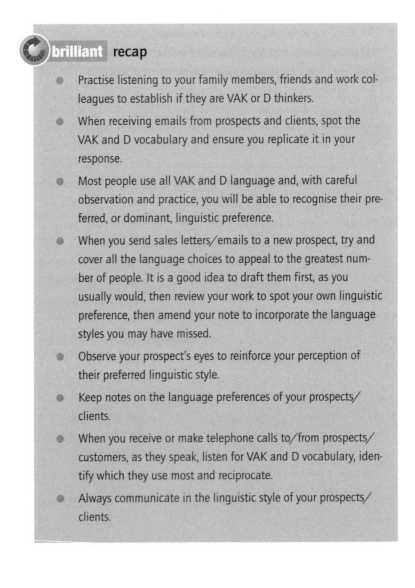

brilliant recap

- Practise listening to your family members, friends and work colleagues to establish if they are VAK or D thinkers.

- When receiving emails from prospects and clients, spot the VAK and D vocabulary and ensure you replicate it in your response.

- Most people use all VAK and D language and, with careful observation and practice, you will be able to recognise their preferred, or dominant, linguistic preference.

- When you send sales letters/emails to a new prospect, try and cover all the language choices to appeal to the greatest number of people. It is a good idea to draft them first, as you usually would, then review your work to spot your own linguistic preference, then amend your note to incorporate the language styles you may have missed.

- Observe your prospect's eyes to reinforce your perception of their preferred linguistic style.

- Keep notes on the language preferences of your prospects/clients.

- When you receive or make telephone calls to/from prospects/customers, as they speak, listen for VAK and D vocabulary, identify which they use most and reciprocate.

- Always communicate in the linguistic style of your prospects/clients.

- Eye movements in the mid and upper planes to your left are a general indicator of an untruth and your prompt to question further.

- Before denoting meaning to eye movements, it is important first to establish if your subject is right or left handed. The eye movements and their significance described here refer only to right-handed individuals and are reversed for those who are left handed.

CHAPTER 13

Parts theory

Halving the objection and embedding a suggestion

'I don't think you could believe
I have a split personality;
we just made it up so you would
think so!'

Anonymous

What is parts therapy?

Psychiatrists and clinical hypnotherapists use parts therapy to resolve inner conflict to modify or change unwanted habits and help people to achieve personal and professional goals. For example, a person suffering from agoraphobia has a part of them wanting to leave their home and experience the outside world and live a 'normal' life, while another part of them is extremely fearful of stepping outside their front door. Similarly, an alcoholic has a part of them that knows they need to abstain, while another part sabotages every effort.

Occasionally, as a result of intense shock or trauma, some people exhibit numerous personalities. The movie *Sybil* presents a thought-provoking example, where Sally Field, as Sybil Dorset, reveals 13 different characters and her life becomes increasingly chaotic as each grows stronger.

In therapy, a health professional engaging a patient suffering from split personality disorder, now referred to as dissociative identity disorder (DID), might say:

> *Therapist* I know that part of you believes A, while another part of you thinks B. That's right, isn't it?

Commercial application for parts theory

Used to overcome sales objections, move conversations forwards and reinforce the benefits of your product or service, parts theory, as we will refer to it throughout the remainder of this chapter, is easily transferred to the business community.

In business development, parts theory is when part of a conflicted prospect clearly recognises the value of your offering and another part then raises an objection or shows uncertainty. In such circumstances, we just assume they are not objecting to everything about your product and our role is to help them recognise and act favourably upon that fact.

If you are coordinating a team in times of change and need to be sure those around you are on board, you might say:

> *A part of you* sees this change as commercially unsettling for everyone, while *another part of you* can see the benefits far exceed the momentary disruption, can't you?

Alternatively, reviewing an individual's sales performance:

> I can appreciate that *part of you* believes you've performed well in the last quarter. *Another part of you,* I know, realises there's room for improvement, isn't there?

Part of you can see how effective parts theory is at melting away objections and bringing the reasons why your prospect will buy your product to the top of the discussion. Another part of you, the intuitive part, already agrees how helpful this technique will be in your daily dealings with clients and prospects.

Basic structure of parts theory

> *Persuader* [A part of you] sees this 'objection/uncertainty'; [another part of you] appreciates the 'advantages/benefits'. Let us explore them.

The following example uses the same phrasal structure, mentioned earlier, to overcome a price objection. We have intensified the response by inserting a combination of different language patterns, which we have marked out and describe in detail.

Persuader [I agree, you are right] [and] I can see how [part of
you] might think this is an expensive option [but,]
you can imagine [another part of you] easily justifying the marginal price increase [can't you?] [because]
of the higher level of service (mention additional
benefits). [This means that] you'll enjoy less downtime, which means greater profitability, and that's
important to you and your company [isn't it?].

The response above incorporates the following selection of language patterns:

The agreement frame

Structure I agree (whatever is said) *and* I'd add that (whatever
you wish to add that moves the dialogue towards
your objective).

The agreement frame is very useful in all kinds of sales negotia-
tion and conflict resolution situations. This simple language pattern turns a potentially negative situation into a positive one.
Have you ever noticed when you agree with someone, even if you
disagree with part of what they say, that it has the effect of taking
the wind out of their sails?

This technique is sometimes compared to ju-jitsu, as metaphori-
cally your opponent's weight is used effectively against them.
Most importantly, it has the effect of reducing resistance as the
'objector' does not detect any opposition to their point of view.
Try this yourself; spend a day agreeing with those around you
when perhaps you might, ordinarily, disagree and observe the
reactions. For our purposes, we use only the first part of the
agreement frame, the agreement statement.

Linguistic mathematics

The linguistic equivalence of addition and subtraction in mathematics is: 'and' and 'but'. The word 'but' subliminally negates

anything that precedes it. The word 'and' adds to and keeps the conversation flowing forwards.

Tag questions

Most of us use these daily without conscious thought. Tag questions are small questions like:

- Don't you? Doesn't it? Didn't it?
- Can't you? Can't it?
- Haven't you? Hasn't it?
- Won't you? Isn't it?

Questions such as these prompt either an audible or inaudible 'yes' from your subject and are even more efficient when you nod your head up to three times as you deliver the question.

Because logic

From childhood, we are programmed to accept whatever follows the word 'because' as a suitable explanation for the question preceding it.

---

brilliant example

Why must I go to bed now?

- Because I say so.
- Because it is bedtime.
- Because you want to grow up big and strong, don't you?

Experiments conducted on the word 'because' conclude that most people more readily comply with a request to change their behaviour if the word 'because' is used in the explanation. Because 'because logic' adds authenticity and credibility, the listener is more likely to concentrate on the statement after the word 'because' and accept it as true.

Complex equivalence

This means that – that means this.

These simple phrases denote 'meaning'; essentially, it is pre-supposed that one event, action or desire *means* another. When we use this technique in a persuasive conversation, we can plant suggestions and create a logical argument where it does not necessarily exist.

 **examples**

- As you are reading this book, you already appreciate the advantage, you will enjoy being more influential and *this means that* you recognise how being more persuasive will change your life in all the ways only you can imagine.
    - The suggestion is clearly that reading this book means you acknowledge how being more persuasive will change your life.
- As you are reading this book, *this means that* you are already imagining how much more persuasive you will be after you have taken part in a Proactive Persuasion Seminar.
    - The suggestion that reading this book means you are already imagining how much more persuasive you will be after taking part in a Proactive Persuasion Seminar.

Returning to the enhanced response, let us look at how each language pattern affects the overall response.

The enhanced response

[I agree, you are right] [and] I can see how [part of you] might think this is an expensive option [but,] you can imagine [another part of you] easily justifying the marginal price increase [can't you?] [because] of the higher level of service (mention additional benefits). [This means that] you'll enjoy less downtime, which means greater profitability, and that's important to you and your company [isn't it?].

The list below clarifies the language pattern used and their intended effect.

Response	Language pattern and effect
I agree, you are right	*Agreement frame* – this removes resistance, making the subject receptive to what follows.
part of you might think this is an expensive option	*Part one of parts theory* – this reduces the importance of the objection, as it is only part of what the subject is questioning.
but	*Linguistic mathematics* – 'but' subliminally negates the part of the objection holding up the sale.
another part of you easily justifying the marginal price increase	*Part two of parts theory* – this leads the prospect towards seeing the advantages of the product/ service.
can't you?	*Tag question* – eliciting a verbal or non-verbal 'yes' response, directing the listener to agree they appreciate the advantages of the product/service.
because	*Because logic* – leads towards the benefits of your product/service and, in this case, it is setting up a complex equivalence.
This means that	*Complex equivalence* – plants the suggestion, pre-supposing one set of benefits means another.
and	*Linguistic mathematics* – 'and' moves the conversation forwards, ensuring the prospect assumes that the additional benefits are significant.
isn't it?	*Tag question* – this initiates a second 'yes' response, audible or otherwise, to the preceding statements.

We began introducing a simple pattern and, I imagine, now you are thinking it has developed into something quite complicated, especially taking into account the additional language patterns we have introduced. To neutralise any fears you may have about making this subject unnecessarily elaborate, remember, it is more than likely you are using, without conscious thought, most of the additional language patterns cited in this chapter. Certainly, you will be after you re-read every word in *Brilliant Persuasion* over again, and again!

brilliant tips

To practise building your confidence we suggest:

● writing down a typical and often repeated objection;

● typing your answers quickly and observe how many language patterns mentioned in this chapter you have used without thought;

● using these patterns proactively;

● reading your written response out loud;

● creating some training scripts; always assume your prospect will find part of your offering attractive.

Whichever way you decide to add parts theory into your sales conversations, the routine we have described illustrates both how the technique works and also how easily it can be combined with other language patterns.

⟳ brilliant recap

- Parts theory initially was used in the world of clinical psychiatry and is easily transferred to the commercial sector.

- Always believe/assume that everyone finds part of your product or service desirable.

- This technique melts away objections and brings the reasons why your prospect will buy your product to the top of the discussion.

- On its own, parts theory is very powerful, yet is easily combined with other language patterns.

Enjoy using parts theory and be confident knowing that only part of you might, at first, be challenged by this; the other part of you, the curious and confident part, can already imagine how easily you will assimilate this technique into your everyday conversations.

CHAPTER 14

The quotes pattern

Plant suggestions without saying a word!

'A fine quotation is a diamond in the hand of a man of wit and a pebble in the hand of a fool.'

Joseph Roux

Why we use quotes to persuade

I remember, after having described how and why we use the quotes pattern to a delegate at a Proactive Persuasion Seminar, he turned and said to me, 'The quotes pattern is the perfect way to place direct and indirect suggestions or embedded commands about your products or services into the minds of others and increase their responsiveness to the messages you want to deliver.' Of course, I agreed.

Structure of the quotes pattern

The quotes pattern is one of the easiest to learn and deliver and, if you are involved in sales marketing and/or business development of any kind, should be high up, if not on the top of, your list of 'must use' persuasive techniques. I recall the person who initially introduced this technique to me, saying, 'The beauty of this technique is that you can quote anyone; create your quotes to fit particular circumstances and even quote non-existent people.' Of course, that is not for me to say, but it was good advice.

Can you start to imagine how you will use this technique in your next presentation? While the quotes pattern is easy to learn and assimilate into conversation, when you begin to use it, there are some subtleties to take into account. The basic structure is straightforward.

Basic structure of the quotes pattern

The person you are quoting + what they have said

We mentioned how it is all right to make up quotes from non-existent people because the issue is not whether or not these people exist; the issue is that you successfully deliver your message in a manner your prospect believes and accepts, isn't it? This means that, to build your confidence using quotes, you should prepare them for your presentation and practise saying them out loud. When you invent quotes, it is not necessary to name your source. Let us look at an example.

Techniques to strengthen quotes

Whenever you want someone to listen, actively mention something apparently said in confidence. In the above example, no one will question who these people are. With quotes, you can say exactly what you want your prospect to think without incrimination because *you* are not saying it.

Persuader   An ex-colleague of mine, now working for the competition, mentioned to me that his manager said to him, in confidence, he thought our products were superior to theirs and he was so fearful of losing market share that they were considering reducing their prices even further.

Obviously, I could not confirm or deny this, but we both know you get what you pay for in this sector, don't you?

Powerful words to use in quotes

● *Most people:* a term that represents the majority, or everybody else other than the person with whom you are talking.

- *Immediately:* have you ever considered when is immediate? It is right away, isn't it? It is now!

For example:

A regular client of mine in your business once said that *most people* who buy this now, *immediately* see the benefits.

Analysing the above quote, you will notice that we are suggesting the prospect should 'buy this now' and to 'immediately see the benefits'. Embedded commands like these bypass the conscious awareness of others, as we are relaying a story about someone else.

The pronoun shift

The pronoun shift is considered by *most people* to be grammatically incorrect, but is often used in everyday conversation without thought. When intentionally used, *you* will easily plant suggestions into your prospect's mind even though initially appearing to be talking about someone else.

When we use a pronoun shift, you start the conversation with words like this:

I	We	The last person
My	Our	Most people
He	She	Some people
They	It	

Then, half-way through the discussion you sneakily direct the emphasis of the conversation towards your subject by using words like you, your and yours.

Examples of pronoun shift:

- The last person that bought this said, 'it was the best investment you'll make because he's made so much money.'
- The last person who bought our product was using the same as you, said, 'The quality of XYZ's product was so poor you'll have to replace them every six months.'

- Most people who've already purchased this insurance policy say, 'It gives you the greatest feeling of security and peace of mind.'
- The last advertiser who took a regular front page advert said, 'You'll be amazed at the level of new business it brought in. Because regular advertising works.'

The pronoun shift is considered by *most people* to be grammatically incorrect but is often used in everyday conversation without thought. When intentionally used, *you* will easily plant suggestions into your prospect's mind even though initially appearing to be talking about someone else.

brilliant examples

- The last person that bought this said, 'It was the best investment *you'll* make because he's made so much money.'
- The last person who bought our product and was using the same as you said, 'The quality of XYZ's product was so poor *you'll* have to replace them every six months.'
- Most people who have already purchased this insurance policy say, 'It gives *you* the greatest feeling of security and peace of mind.'
- The last advertiser who took a regular front page advert said, '*You'll* be amazed at the level of new business it brought in. Because regular advertising works.'

Quoting a real person

Occasionally, a well-known person in your industry might say something quotable. Vigilantly follow the press, trade journals, events and conferences for speakers and compile a list of helpful quotes from influential people. You never know, even a politician might say something to promote your cause!

Quotes have the effect of quietening our conscious minds, enabling us to communicate directly with the subconscious minds of
others. This pattern allows you to say almost anything you wish
because you are quoting someone else. You should keep your
quote within the context of your conversation and, because you
are saying something apparently said by another person, your
prospect will not express resistance towards you.

brilliant recap

- Use a pronoun shift to redirect the crucial part of any statement towards your prospect.

- Embed commands into your quotes.

- Use the quotes pattern to say what you want your prospects to
  think.

- Quote anyone and create quotes to fit particular circumstances.

- As a guide, follow this pattern: the name of the person you're
  quoting + what they said + (optional) I/you shift.

- The quotes pattern enables you to place direct and indirect suggestions about your products/services into your prospect's
  mind.

- Whenever you want someone to listen actively, mention something said in confidence.

- When making up quotes and, indeed, in general conversation,
  use the phrases 'most people' and 'immediately' as often as
  you can.

- Follow influential people in your industry; read the trade press
  for quotes that help your cause.

- If you decide to quote others, remember you do not have to be
  word perfect and the quotes do not have to be attributed to
  anyone, as long as your message is relayed, and the suggestion
  received.

CHAPTER 15

Persuasive body language

Command attention with non-verbal communication

'What you do speaks so loud that I cannot hear what you say.'

Ralph Waldo Emerson

Why is body language important?

In this chapter, you discover the meaning of the subtle gestures and movements that your prospects and/or clients make while you engage them in conversation or are making a presentation to them. The insight you will gain from observing your prospect's body language will give you tremendous understanding about what they are unconsciously saying and feeling, and enable you to enhance your charisma, tailor your presentations more accurately, lower resistance, build rapport and increase their level of responsiveness to you and your message.

As well as learning to be acutely aware of the subliminal messages revealed by others, you will learn how to moderate your body language proactively to ensure, on an unconscious level, those meeting you feel comfortable in your presence.

A book on the subject of persuasion would be incomplete without reference to the unconscious, involuntary movements we make as we engage others in conversation.

Body language is a vast topic; entire books are devoted to it alone. For our purpose we review a small selection of movements occasionally referred to as 'tells' that you can use, and we reveal others you may choose to avoid.

Re-engineering your social status

Let us be clear; being perceived at a higher status than your prospect, colleague, client, or even your boss, might not always be a good idea. Equally, being considered of a lower status can be detrimental to your success. Before purposefully manipulating your perceived status level with the techniques revealed here, be mindful of others and, whatever situation you are in, determine the most appropriate level required to benefit you the most.

With tiny changes to your body language, you can alter how others perceive you both consciously and subconsciously. By changing your physiology, that is, acting as if you are more confident than you feel, others will view you as being self-assured and, curiously, you will become more confident. Fake it to make it.

You would be wise never to underestimate your prospect's innate capacity to read the subliminal 'tells' you are unknowingly revealing. They may not be able to interpret what they consciously observe, but they will, undoubtedly, 'feel' a certain way about being in your company as a consequence of your body language. The information you are about to discover will empower you to be able to purposefully enhance the personal impact you have on others as we concentrate our attention on the movements of the hands, eyes and the head.

The hands

I wonder how much attention you pay to your hand movements when you speak?

Palms down

Figure 15.1 Palms down
Source: Tom Merton/Getty Images.

When we talk with our palms facing down, we are showing to others we have a high level of personal confidence, which is a good thing. In a worst case scenario, with excessive use, others may consider you bossy and/or controlling.

While you are progressively building rapport and making an active effort to lay down the foundations to most efficiently deliver your sales message, if your habit is to present with your palms down, counter-intuitively and without awareness, you could be creating subliminal resistance.

The message is to be confident, of course, while tempering signs of overconfidence by occasionally revealing your palms as you speak. Should you notice your prospect's palms mostly in this downward position as they speak, you'll know they are confident, possibly controlling, and maybe used to having their way.

 **tip**

If your prospect communicates mostly with their palms down, their personality type might be controlling. Should you observe this, adapt your approach to harmonise with theirs.

Palms up

Figure 15.2   Palms up
Source: ASDF_MEDIA/Shutterstock

Openly revealing your palms as you speak is a brilliant gesture to adopt proactively because to whomever you are talking, it subconsciously relays a message of openness and signals you to be a trustworthy, honest person wanting your message to be accepted and believed. It is not a display of status, power, authority or confidence unlike the palms down position.

If you notice your prospect displaying this palms up 'tell', they are keen for you to accept and understand what they are saying. Should they reveal a preference to communicate with their palms up, often, they may find themselves explaining themselves to others and lack authority or confidence in some way. Once you recognise this, adapt your approach appropriately.

☀ brilliant tip

If you mostly adopt palms up gestures as you speak, start interspersing slightly more palms down movements as you speak to reveal, on a subconscious level, to others that you are confident and in control as well as being open and likeable.

Finger-pinch hold

Figure 15.3   Finger-pinch hold
Source: Marcos Mesa/Sam Wordley/Shutterstock.

If you attend sales training seminars or, indeed, any event where you have to listen to a professionally trained speaker, you will notice the occasional use of the finger-pinch hold. This powerful hand gesture suggests confidence and that you are speaking with genuine knowledge and authority. It can also be used purposefully to direct attention to especially important points you are making verbally.

If your prospect adopts this hand gesture, they are signalling confidence, authority and status, especially when combined with the palms-down position mentioned earlier.

brilliant tip

Develop the habit of using a finger-pinch hold whenever you wish to emphasise particular points in your presentation and start to combine palms down/up gestures deliberately as you speak. Be careful not to overuse these hand movements, as you run the risk of either appearing aggressively overconfident and brash or insecure and requiring acceptance. Always show sensitivity towards your prospect by adapting your body language to ensure others feel comfortable around you.

Cautionary note about the finger pinch

The finger pinch is an accepted hand movement for Europeans and Americans. However, in Brazil it has rather negative connotations. We will leave it to you to research its meaning.

Hands close to the mouth

Figure 15.4   Hands close to the mouth
Source: wavebreakmedia/Shutterstock

Next time you are talking to a prospect, notice whether they unconsciously move their hands towards their mouth. This can be a sign that they:

- are thinking/evaluating what you are saying;
- want to speak, but they are curbing their desire to do so. Observing this movement may prompt you to pause a moment and allow your subject to talk. If they do not, they are either still refraining from doing so or evaluating what you are saying;
- know they have said something not entirely factual if simultaneously you notice the upward movement of their eyes to your left. Take this is your cue to ask more probing questions.

Steeple position

You may see those in authority or of high status using the steeple position hand gesture, as it is a powerful indicator of confidence and self-assurance. Should your prospect assume this stance, you will know you are, potentially, dealing with someone with a high

Figure 15.5 Steeple position
Source: Hinterhaus Productions/Getty Images

level of self-confidence, knowledgeable in their field and used to commanding respect.

You may send others the same message about yourself by adopting this hand gesture. To be convincing, though, you must also remember those of higher status tend to move less. If you are someone who moves your head, hands and arms often and rapidly, this gesture will appear incongruous and you will be transmitting to others the opposite message to your intention.

Hand clench

Figure 15.6   Hand clench
Source: PhotoAlto/Eric Audras/Getty Images.

This is a very revealing tell. The fingers are not always intertwined, as shown in Figure 15.6; the hands may be observed one on top of the other. Initially, you might believe it gives the impression of confidence, especially because those doing it often smile.

Hands clenched in this manner or one on top of the other can indicate a restrained, anxious or negative attitude. In a sales setting, the person adopting this hand configuration may be holding something back, feeling anxious or unconvincing and failing to negotiate effectively.

Eye contact and head movements

The right eye link for developing deeper rapport

Most people are mindful of the significance of maintaining non-threatening eye contact with customers and prospects. Now we are going to take eye contact up a level in a way you may not have considered.

While the neuroscience community does not accept the concept of left dominant, right dominant personality, it agrees that each side of the brain controls different functions. For example, language is a left brain function and attention is a right brain function.

When we think of attention, we think of concentration, thought, awareness, interest and consideration.

To enhance rapport and create deeper connections with others, access the right hemisphere of their brain by lining up your right eye with theirs. When you try this, it is easier if you position yourself a little to the left of your subject. You will be amazed at the effect it has.

Eye blocking or squinting

If you ask a question and your prospect subtly squints their eyes, they are subconsciously trying to block that question, and their response may be untruthful. This is called eye blocking.

Squinting can also be seen while someone is reading something disagreeable. It will happen instantaneously without his or her awareness and is a very useful 'tell' when negotiating contracts or devising plans.

brilliant tip

If you see your prospect squinting slightly, following a question, and you have ruled out the sun is in their eyes, progress cautiously with the knowledge you have gleaned and try to corroborate what they have said later in your meeting.

Head nodding

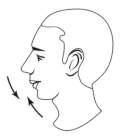

Figure 15.7 Head nodding

Nodding the head at the point of asking a question helps to elicit a positive response covertly. Adopt this habit moderately, for obvious reasons, to remove resistance and make others responsive to you and your message.

brilliant tip

Practise nodding your head three times as you look at your prospect in the right eye when asking tag questions, such as: Can't it? Won't it? Doesn't it? Hasn't it? Won't you? Don't you? Isn't it? Aren't you? You will discover, in most cases, the person with whom you are talking will automatically nod their head in agreement, even if they disagree.

Head tilting

Tilting the head to the side can indicate a sign of interest, sometimes curiosity or query, especially if the head moves forwards at the same time. Should you see your client tilting their head and simultaneously moving backwards, however, this can indicate uncertainty or suspicion.

Figure 15.8   Head tilting
Source: Compassionate Eye Foundation/David Oxberry/Getty Images.

brilliant tip

As you listen to your prospect speaking, tilt your head slightly to the left or right at an appropriate moment to imply, subliminally to them, that you are interested in what they are saying. This will deepen rapport, remove resistance and increase responsiveness.

Keeping your head still

We have mentioned head nodding and tilting; some of us tend to move our heads too often when speaking. When the head is still or moved slowly, it can show that a person is serious, confident and authoritative. Continuously moving one's head with constant ducking and darting eye movements indicates someone under threat and of a lesser status.

When the head remains still, it is easier to observe others with the right eye link. Curiously, by holding your head in a fixed position or moving slowly, others will perceive you as someone of higher status and seniority than maybe you are.

Head movements and the truth

When a person responds to a question or statement and shakes their head either positively or negatively *as they speak,* the likelihood is they are being truthful. On the other hand, if the head movement occurs slightly *later than the speech,* there is a possibility that what they are saying is untrue and, again, this is your prompt to investigate further.

The eyebrow raise

Figure 15.9   The eyebrow raise
Source: PhotoAlto/Eric Audras/Getty Images.

Raising the eyebrows to others indicates you are friendly and open and, therefore, confident. It is a clear way of asking for attention from others. If you move your head slowly on a single plane, then look at someone while raising your eyebrows, you are demanding attention and a response.

Meeting others

Charismatic, confident people meet others in their space. It is vital to be client-focused so, when meeting someone for the first time, step forward first to shake their hand, not the other way round.

brilliant recap

- Limit how often your hands are face down when making presentations, to avoid being thought of as controlling.

- Allow your palms to face up occasionally to appear open and trustworthy.

- Pinch your thumb and first finger to direct attention to particular points (do not do this in Brazil).

- Keep your hands away from your mouth; observe whether your prospect has this habit.

- Steeple your hands; this signals a high level of confidence.

- Do not clench your fingers.

- Nod your head three times to elicit yes responses when asking questions.

- Tilt your head to show interest. If your prospect does this, you know they are at least curious.

- Line your right eye to the right eye of your prospect, to deepen rapport.

- Move your head slowly.

- Raising your eyebrows reveals you as friendly and open and, when combined with slow head movements, will command attention.

PART 3

Persuasive questioning technique

f you Google 'questioning technique', over 32 million results will invade your screen. If you funnel down and search for 'questioning methodology appropriate for sales professionals', you will discover a further 18 million plus articles. Apparently, a lot is written about this very popular area of persuasion. The crucial questions most people ask that I would like you to mull over as you read further are:

- What is important to you about being able to ask persuasive questions?
- What is the single, most significant advantage that being able to ask compelling, persuasive questions will make to you, personally?

While pondering over those questions, it is important to recognise that the asking of questions is more than a process of merely eliciting relevant information to drive you forwards, towards your sale. Never forget, your prospect is more likely to have an interest in, or purchase your product or service as a consequence of how *they* think about it, and not how you think about it. Precisely formed questions expertly articulated will enable you to plant proactively purchasing suggestions and thoughts into your prospect's mind that they believe are theirs and that guide them to make mutually beneficial buying decisions.

Properly constructed questions will:

- positively affect how your prospect thinks about your product or service;
- form the basis for developing persuasive dialogue;
- heighten your level of influence.

Always remember that questions are your ultimate persuasive tool. The more proficient you are at asking them, the easier it will become for you to sell. Consider this: the mind cannot not answer a question; had you ever thought about that before? When you pose a question, the listener or reader automatically searches for the answer; it is entirely automatic. This is as powerful as it is intriguing because, simply by asking questions, you are exercising control over someone else's mind and their thinking and, because of this, asking questions is more powerful than responding to them. To quote Voltaire: 'Judge a man by his questions rather than his answers.'

Whoever asks the questions is the leader. Do not be hijacked. In this part, we will reveal a selection of different question types that you will use to plant ideas and suggestions into the minds of others and to lead them to think what you want them to think. Also, to ensure you are fully prepared for future sales meetings, because the process of persuasion originates inside you, we will introduce an assortment of questions devised specifically to intensify your level of focus towards the outcome you seek and create within you a 'mindset' for persuasion.

We will concentrate on the following types of questions:

- Pre-suppositional
- Tag
- Powerful
- Future pacing
- Criteria

CHAPTER 16

Pre-suppositional questions

Make it easy for your prospects by generously providing them with the answers you want

'We get wise by asking questions, and even if these are not answered, we get wise, for a well-packed question carries its answer on its back as a snail carries its shell.'

James Stephens

What is important to you about formulating powerful pre-suppositional questions?

One of the simplest means to enhance and develop your persuasive skills with your colleagues, prospects and clients is to modify your language slightly and one of the smartest ways to achieve this is to integrate pre-suppositions into your speech.

It is challenging to frame a question that is not pre-suppositional because most are, and we ask them unconsciously because it is second nature. Think about this: rather than asking questions to merely acquire information, what advantages do you imagine you will enjoy by proactively planting pre-suppositions into your questions and everyday conversation? In this chapter, you will learn how to place pre-suppositions intentionally into your speech and, by doing so, guide your prospect to accept as true what you want them to believe.

What is special about pre-suppositional questions?

Pre-suppositional questions have within them concepts and ideas the listener must accept as true before they can consider offering a response. As persuaders, we use this technique to communicate assumptions and to lead and assist our prospects to respond to our enquiries in a manner that we control and desire. Mostly, we want our prospects to think what we want them to think.

Below are some examples of pre-suppositional questions.

brilliant examples

Example 1

Persuader   What is your favourite persuasive technique in this book?

Pre-suppositions   You have a preferred persuasive technique and it is included in *Brilliant Persuasion*.

Example 2

Persuader   When you finish reading this book, with which of your colleagues will you share some of the persuasive techniques you have learnt?

Pre-suppositions   You will read every chapter of *Brilliant Persuasion*, you have acquired some persuasive techniques, you have colleagues and you will share some information.

How are pre-suppositional questions helpful?

- Because most people are averse to making decisions, our use of pre-suppositions enables us to help them make unconscious decisions of agreement, more quickly!

- As persuaders, sometimes we have our demons and doubts, the little voice inside whispering, 'What if they reject our offer?' Carefully prepared and positioned pre-suppositional questions and statements enable us to bypass the 'Are you interested' part of a presentation, enabling us to progress straight to the, 'What part of our product/service interests you most?' part. As the conversation progresses, we identify more with our prospect and discover more about their needs.

Below are further examples of pre-suppositional questions.

brilliant examples

After a sales presentation	Which particular areas of my presentation interested you most?
Pre-supposition	There are particular areas of interest.
Supplier to client	Looking ahead to the next financial year, what additional products are you going to include in your portfolio?
Pre-supposition	It is presumed that the contract will be renewed for the next fiscal year and other products will be included.
With a prospect	What is most important to you about working with a consultancy like XYZ?
Pre-supposition	There is something specific the prospect appreciates when retaining a new consultancy and it is presumed that the two parties will be working together.
With your line manager	What part of my performance has been particularly effective in the past month?
Pre-supposition	It is assumed that part of his/her performance was outstanding in the previous month and the line manager noticed.
With a market trader	What discount are you going to offer me on this today?
Pre-supposition	It is presumed that a discount will be offered today!

Not all questions need to be answered

As you learn more about pre-suppositions, you will appreciate how difficult it is to ask a question that is not pre-suppositional. Sometimes, we make pre-suppositional statements deliberately, in the form of questions solely to plant suggestions to move the conversation forwards to the next topic.

---

brilliant example

Persuader   I wonder when the next outage will happen? If you do not upgrade your systems soon, moving on, I'd like you to see how XYZ fits with your objectives for that department...

In the above example, spoken conversationally, the persuader is not seeking a response; the idea is planted in the prospect's mind that something will or could go wrong, should the systems not be upgraded soon.

brilliant tip

As well as asking questions to draw information from your prospect, start constructing pre-suppositional questions to lead your prospect towards your outcome. Begin by thinking about what you want to happen and communicate it in a manner that assumes it will.

For example, instead of asking your customer:

Persuader Do you think this could be useful?

(your prospect will respond either 'yes' or 'no' or, if they wish to be kind, may elaborate) construct your query in such a way that they have to respond actively, like this:

Persuader What's the most significant way you see this product/
service being useful to you/your company?

To answer this question, the prospect must start a mental journey
inward, that you have initiated, as they visualise in their mind's
eye the most significant way your product/service will be useful.

The question pre-supposes that there are particularly useful
aspects of your product/service they will find valuable. In this
example, the persuader is actively directing the customer to think
what he/she wants them to think by asking a question that effectively commands them to: 'see this product being useful'.

The persuader does not have to identify how his/her product will
be of interest; the prospect is doing this. Whatever the customer
says will be right and unique to them. Once they inform you,
tailor your presentation to their individual requirements.

brilliant tip

Focus on the outcome you seek and plan your questions to ensure
you always get the answer you want.

Consider these questions, which we asked you to consider in the
introduction to this part of the book:

● What is important to you about being able to ask persuasive
  questions?

    - In the first example, it is pre-supposed that you find
      something important about asking pre-suppositional
      questions and, as soon as you think about answering,
      you have already agreed with the premise.

● What is the single, most significant advantage being able to
  ask compelling, persuasive questions will make to you,
  personally?

- In the second example, it is presumed that being more persuasive has a single significant advantage that means something personally. By answering this question, you have agreed with this pre-supposition.

Both questions allude to the same thing:

How to make pre-suppositional questions even more irresistible

To enhance pre-suppositional questions, let us look at 'awareness patterns'. These are a small set of words in the English language implying awareness and, compellingly, everything said after them is pre-suppositional as being true. When we use these words to describe the benefits of any product or service, the *only* open question is your prospect's 'awareness' of the advantages of your offering.

● notice;

● see;

● realise;

● aware;

● experience;

● discover.

When embedded in questions, awareness vocabulary creates assertions like:

● Did you notice that . . . ?

● Were you aware that . . . ?

● Had you realised that . . . ?

This focuses the listener's mind towards considering if they had noticed, were aware or had realised that something was happening and they concentrate less upon the overall truth of the statement.

When we embed assertions into questions, they are less likely to be challenged and far more persuasive than when given directly.

brilliant examples

● Have you *realised* how much more successful you will be once you start using pre-suppositional questions?

  – It is presumed you will be more successful when you begin using pre-suppositional questions. The only question is whether you have realised how much more successful you will be.

● When you integrate our accounting software, you will *discover* how easily and efficiently your team will produce the balances and reports you need, to see how your business is doing.

  – It is presumed you will integrate the new accounting software and your team will produce the data you seek more easily. The only question is when you want to discover this.

● Are you *aware* that when you migrate your portfolio to us, you will *realise* how our commitment to tailored solutions will massively increase your yield?

  – It is presumed the prospect will migrate their portfolio and the yield will increase. The open questions are if they realise this and if they are aware this will happen.

brilliant recap

  ● Use carefully prepared pre-suppositional questions to direct and influence the thinking of your customers.

  ● Pre-suppositional questions help your prospect to make decisions more quickly!

- Pre-suppositional questions move sales conversations towards discussing benefits and not interest level.

- Integrating the vocabulary of internal representations and awareness will enhance your pre-suppositional questions and statements.

- Use pre-suppositional questions to plant ideas and identify specific areas of interest in your products or services.

- Answers are not always required.

Deployed wisely, a planned, pre-suppositional questioning technique will substantially enhance your persuasive powers in ways only you can imagine.

CHAPTER 17

Tag questions

Gain spontaneous agreement

'If you do not ask the right questions, you do not get the right answers. A question asked in the right way often points to its own answer.'

Edward Hodnett

f there was a language pattern that effortlessly encouraged your prospects or clients to think or say 'yes' and instil positive feelings about the services and the products you are promoting, it is very likely you would use it, wouldn't you?

If, just this second, you thought 'yes', apart from the fact that the above idea is, of course, desirable, the phrase 'wouldn't you?' at the close of the question led you more easily to accede to the overall message.

Tag questions like 'wouldn't you?' are small questions designed to coax the listener to agree unconsciously, verbally or nonverbally, to your statements while inviting them to verify their understanding of what you have said. They are a function of everyday conversation; everyone uses them mostly without conscious awareness, but, when used proactively, they are deceptively persuasive.

Listeners and readers find this type of question almost impossible to oppose. If your prospect nods their head as you deliver the tag question, you have succeeded in creating an internal 'yes set' in their mind. The extraordinary thing is, occasionally, even if you have stated something you had not expected your prospect to accept, you will, nevertheless, see them nodding their head instinctively in agreement, such is the power of this pattern.

Example tag questions

These small questions placed at the end of statements are deceptively powerful in gaining agreement from your prospect and do not always have to be answered.

Don't you?	Will you?	Won't you?
Aren't you?	Can't you?	Wouldn't you?
Couldn't you?	Shouldn't you?	Has he/she?
Haven't you?	Isn't it?	May I?
Didn't I?	Would you?	Must I?

If you want to learn about the correct way to formulate tag questions, there are some guidelines at the end of this chapter. However, it is important to not become over-involved with the technicalities of English grammar, as most of us follow these rules unconsciously.

brilliant tip

Observe when others automatically, without thought, add tag questions in their speech, particularly when they are talking to you, and notice how they make you feel. Listen carefully to the response you receive from others as they respond to your tag questions. Imagine how much more persuasive you will be when you start to use this simple technique purposefully.

Enhancing the effectiveness of tag questions

We can quantum leap the impact asking tag questions has on others by adding and combining three additional, somewhat covert, components:

- embedded commands;
- intonation;
- body language.

Embedded commands

Let us clarify what we mean by an embedded command and why we use them.

An embedded command is a suggestion not discernible by the conscious. If you give a direct command to someone to do or think about something in a particular way, they may reject your proposal or, in some instances, follow the opposite path. When, however, a command suggestion is given while you appear to be talking about something else, it slips unnoticed past conscious awareness directly into the least resistant subconscious part of the listener's brain and, eventually, surfaces as their idea.

You may think this sounds complicated but, by now, because you have read quite a lot about both tag questions and embedded commands, we expect you can see how effective this combination of techniques can be, can't you?

This combination of delivering a subliminal command suggestion while asking a tag question is a highly useful grouping of patterns and is amazingly efficient and imperceptible from your prospect's viewpoint.

Before we offer further examples, let us review the earlier paragraph:

> *Persuader* You may think this sounds complicated but, by now, because you have read quite a lot about both tag questions and embedded commands, we expect you can see how effective this combination of techniques can be, can't you?

Notice the linguistic ambiguity and embedded command to '*by now*' or '*buy now*'. Most people will not hear the command in this context, as we are implying the passage of time. Effectively, we have commanded our prospect to 'buy now' and they have said 'yes' to the entire statement, which refers to something entirely different.

Example embedded commands

The best commands are always short, usually a maximum of four words; the following list provides an idea of some generic suggestions you can use.

Buy now	Like this	Like me
Sign up	Start now	Want this
Work with me/Co. name	See the potential	Try this
Call me		

---

brilliant examples

Imagine you are talking to a prospect and have gleaned some basic information. You might say:

> That's right. So, I understand you might be interested in XYZ aspect of our product/service, mightn't you?

The command integrated into this statement is 'be interested'. You spotted it, didn't you?

Identify the embedded commands in the following tag questions:

- It's a good idea to try this, don't you think?
- This price structure works for you, doesn't it?
- I believe you like the idea of being able to do this now, don't you?
- The team's performance will improve when you integrate our system, won't it?
- Ultimately, you know you will achieve more with this, don't you?

Each of the examples above contains a suggestion favourable to the product and each question commands a 'yes' answer.

Intonation

The second element ensuring tag questions and embedded commands are compelling is your tone of voice. The secret is to assume a lower tone of voice and to deliver the question at a slightly slower speed. Should you take on an upward inflection, you will appear to be seeking validation of the points you have raised, not asserting them as fact.

brilliant tip

An upward voice inflection will, unintentionally, always imply uncertainty. Should you recognise this speech style as your own, to be effective as a persuader, practise reversing it and adopting a downward commanding inflection.

Body language

The third factor that will quantum leap the overall effectiveness of this pattern, and embeds the information you are giving even further, involves your body language. As you deliver the tag question, lock eyes with your subject and subtly nod your head three times.

This nodding of the head, the hypnotic nod, as it is called, is contagious, a little like yawning, and is one of the subtlest and most powerful influencing tools you can add to your growing treasure chest of techniques.

Practise this little pattern and you will be amazed at how easily you will be able to gain your prospect's agreement and plant suggestions.

Follow these rules for the correct formulation of tag questions

These are the ground rules for forming the two-word tag questions. Please do not dwell on these; you are already an expert.

● Your chosen subject in the statement must be the same as in the tag question.

● The verbs in both statement and tag question must match.

● The tag question is usually negative if your comment is positive and vice versa.

● If you place present and past simple tenses in positive statements, typically the auxiliary verb is omitted. However, the auxiliaries 'does', 'do' or 'did' are used. If you use a negative statement in the past simple or present tense, the auxiliaries do not: didn't or doesn't will be present automatically.

● When using the 'there is' structure, 'is' is reflected in the tag.

● If 'no one', 'somebody' or 'something' is the main subject in a statement, it is used in the tag.

● Refer to nothing or something; 'they' is used in the tag when referring to somebody or someone.

brilliant recap

● Tag questions are small questions placed at the end of sentences used to elicit agreement.

● Practise building tag questions into your sales presentation and say them out loud. Test them with friend and family without indicating what you are doing and gauge their response.

● Embedding suggestions into your tag questions is a particularly powerful persuasion technique.

● Look into your prospect's eyes and nod your head three times as you deliver the tag question.

● Use tag questions often until they become second nature.

CHAPTER 18

Powerful questions

Open your prospect's mind, stimulate curiosity and covertly plant suggestions

'It is not the answer that enlightens but the question.'

Eugène Ionesco

In this chapter, we identify what makes some questions more powerful than others; we show how to use questions to plant suggestions and lead your prospects to think precisely what you want them to think. Also, we consider if there is ever a good time or reason to ask closed questions and, if there is, when to do so.

All questions are not equal

The American Educational Psychologist Benjamin Bloom (1913–99) classified questions into six progressively more sophisticated levels known as Bloom's Hierarchy of Questions. Here is a summary of his scheme:

Level	Question type	What this question type requires
One	Knowledge-based	The recognition, gathering and recall of information
Two	Comprehension	Thinking at a lower level and the communication of knowledge without verbatim repetition
Three	Application	Applying learnt information to other situations to solve and explain problems
Four	Analysis	Systematically examining facts and information to resolve challenges
Five	Synthesis	The use of original creative thinking to identify solutions
Six	Evaluation	The assessment of good or not so good

Level one, knowledge-based questions, is the first and simplest of questioning techniques used for gathering information. After the poet and writer Rudyard Kipling (1865–1936) wrote a short poem about them, they also became known as Kipling Questions. Here is his poem:

I keep six honest serving men (They taught me all I knew); Their names are What and Why and When and How and Where and Who.

Questions beginning with these words are naturally open, have varying degrees of effectiveness and elicit different forms of information.

Open questions

Starting questions with the following words will ensure they are open, pre-suppositional and powerful.

Less powerful questions		← - - - - - - - - - - - - →		More powerful questions
Which	Who	When	How	What/What if

Questions starting with 'How' tend to be assumptive and those beginning with 'What' elicit more thoughtful replies. 'What if' lead questions are an alternative way of directing your prospect to 'imagine' something and reflect before answering, and are very powerful indeed.

Closed questions

Closed questions elicit yes/no responses and can begin with the words below; this is by no means an exhaustive list.

Do	Could	Would	Can	Are	Will

When to use closed questions

It is always preferable to start a meeting by asking open questions, gradually progressing towards those requiring a narrower response, and finally asking closed questions. Open questions appear less threatening and generate lots of information; they help build rapport and direct the conversation towards your goal.

As your prospect becomes comfortable responding to open exploratory questions, start asking more directed pre-suppositional ones that include the vocabulary of both internal representation and awareness.

Vocabulary of internal representation
The following words purposely compel listeners and readers to begin a mental journey of imagination. Whatever they have imagined is unique to them.

- Consider/considered
- Contemplate for a moment
- Think about/thought about
- What if
- What is it like when Imagine/Imagined
- Ponder
- Reflect on

Vocabulary of awareness
When referring to awareness patterns, we mean a small set of words in the English language that imply knowledge and, compellingly, everything said after them is pre-supposed to be true. When you use these words to describe the benefits of any product or service, the *only* open question is your prospect's 'awareness' of the advantages of your offering.

Notice	See/seen	Realise
Aware	Experience	Discover

Using this lexis helps your prospect to take mental ownership of your product or service at an early stage in your meeting.
Towards the end of your presentation, asking closed questions will clarify requirements and gain commitment.

🔘 **brilliant** examples

Powerful questions

The questions below are those a sales professional might ask a potential client. They are all powerful, requiring thoughtful answers. By reading them often, you can, perhaps, absorb the vocabulary, imagine your sales environment and tailor this questioning format to your business and individual style.

1   What are you seeking to achieve here?

Response We need to streamline this department to cut costs and increase productivity. Also, we have a problem with uniformity of service delivery.

Analysis This is a broad, powerful 'What lead' opening question, structured to yield as much information as possible. It is also *pre-suppositional* because it presumes the prospective client is seeking to achieve something.

2   What did you first *notice* to make you *realise* you need XYZ?

Response Our IT services were not uniform across the company and the department was haemorrhaging money because we had overused costly contractors.

Analysis This powerful 'What lead' question seeks further information and uses the vocabulary of *awareness*, the words *notice* and *realise*. This question is *pre-suppositional*, as it is assumed something was seen and the prospect understands something is needed. It also contains an embedded suggestion, 'you need XYZ'. (where XYZ is your product, service or company).

3   Can you *imagine* continuing like this much longer?

Response No, not really, because . . .

Analysis This closed question uses the vocabulary of *internal representation*. The word 'Imagine' instructs the prospect to imagine the impact of carrying on as they are and the negative response confirms they would prefer not to.

4   How do you *see* our products satisfying your requirements?

Response They will enable us to achieve 90 per cent automation of our
department by Q4 and savings of 75 per cent.

Analysis   This is an *assumptive question*, as it begins with the word 'how'
and it uses the vocabulary of *awareness* with the word 'see'. The
prospect is invited to 'see' how the products offered will satisfy
their needs. A prospect might say, 'I was rather hoping you would
tell me', which would be a fantastic answer. The sales professional
may continue with, 'Of course, tell me, what do you need to
achieve here?' And so the dialogue progresses.

5   Do you need to cut costs now?

Response Yes, because . . .

Analysis   A *closed question*, beginning with the word 'do' elicits a 'yes'
response and acclimatises the client in this example to saying yes.
It also conceals the embedded suggestion, 'cut costs now'.

6   Do you need to start the process within the next five months?

Response Yes, because . . .

Analysis   This *closed question* elicits a 'yes' response and conceals the
embedded suggestion, 'start the process'.

**7   Which of our solutions most interests you? Is it A + description or B
    + description?**

Response Both seem good, though option B will mostly satisfy our
requirements.

Analysis   This is a powerful classic, closing *pre-suppositional* question,
assuming that one of the solutions offered will interest the prospect. However, use with care and only if the context is right. Prospects are very savvy and this is a very obvious close.

> ### ✦ brilliant tip
>
> Follow open questions with closed questions. Use closed questions to lead your prospect to reaffirm crucial points, positive and negative, that they have already stated.

How to deepen rapport while asking closed questions

Occasionally, when posing closed questions, you will elicit either a 'yes because' or a 'no because' answer. The words people use after they say 'because' are critical because they reveal something about your subject even they will not know. Once you know what to look for, you will be able to identify whether your prospect is motivated either *towards* an objective or *away* from a problem to achieve a goal.

This is vital information to anyone needing to persuade. However motivated, each group expresses themselves using distinctly different vocabulary when talking about areas of significant interest. For Brilliant Persuaders, this is yet another method to enable you to speak the language of your prospects and, in so doing, deepen rapport, reduce resistance and raise responsiveness.

Towards-oriented vocabulary: towards-oriented people frequently express themselves using the following vocabulary:

Accomplish	Achieve	Advantages	Benefits
Collect	Enable	Get	Have
Obtain	Reap	Secure	Win

Away-oriented vocabulary: away-oriented people favour words from this group:

Abolish	Avoid	Eliminate
Eradicate	Exclude	Fix
Get rid of	Have to deal with	It's not perfect
Prevent	Remove	Solve
Stop	Won't have to	

Below are two examples of how the same question can be answered differently, depending on *motivational direction*:

1   Do you need to cut costs now?

Response Yes, because when we reduce costs, our profit margins will increase, ultimately enabling the company to grow and secure greater market share.

Analysis The use of the words 'enabling' and 'secure' indicate that this response comes from a *towards-oriented* individual.

2   Do you need to cut costs now?

Response Oh, yes, because they are escalating, we have to remove the excess and stop them spiralling out of control before it's too late. Otherwise, we'll have to deal with closure and redundancies. We cannot keep going like this.

Analysis The same question can produce an entirely different answer. The words 'remove', 'stop' and 'deal with' tell us this response comes from an *away-oriented* individual.

In a work environment, 40 per cent of people are away-oriented and 40 per cent are towards-oriented; 20 per cent are both. Once you have identified the vocabulary set used by your prospect, continue your conversation using their lexis. This artful and subtle technique deepens rapport and seamlessly places you on the same wavelength as your prospect.

Embedding suggestions into questions

When we ask questions, we actively control the degree of flexibility we offer our prospects to formulate their responses; effectively, we are scoping their reply.

Powerful questions accomplish much more than purely eliciting information; they become powerfully persuasive when embedded commands, suggestions and the response we seek are covertly concealed within them, thus guiding the conversation forward towards the subjects we wish our customer to think about and discuss. To accomplish this, it is essential at the outset to identify the suggestions you want to embed and then carefully construct your question around them.

To illustrate this, we have inserted some simple, mostly generic commands into the following questions:

Suggestion   Question

Live in this   What might you change if you could live in this
house   house, now?

Analysis An estate agent could use this question. The scope of the response is pre-determined. In this particular *pre-suppositional question*, it is presumed that the potential purchaser would change something if they were to live in the house. When the client responds with what they might change, they have imagined themselves living there. The phrase 'live in this house' is an *embedded command*, given as a message to the subconscious to do just that!

Remember, the subconscious mind is the route of least resistance and will ruminate upon this command, without conscious awareness. The agent could, similarly, say, 'This is a fantastic location. If I could live in this house now, I'd extend the kitchen, wouldn't you?' This is ingenious, because the client's subconscious mind picks up, 'I could live in this house now, I'd extend the kitchen'. The *tag question*, 'wouldn't you?' invites agreement and the *pronoun shift* 'I/you' transfers everything said before it onto the client.

Suggestion   Question

Ready to buy Before you are ready to buy now what further
information can I offer you?

Analysis On face value, this apparently straightforward question appears to invite the prospect to request further information before completing the purchase. It is covertly suggesting to the potential purchaser that they are 'ready to buy now'. Note the positioning of the word 'now'. Is it at the end of the phrase, 'ready to buy now' or at the beginning of the phrase 'now what further information'? Alternatively, the sales professional might say, 'Before you are ready to make your decision, now what further information can I offer you?'

Suggestion	Question
Buy this	What difference would it make if by this time next week you have a new security system?

Analysis This simple question suggests the prospect think about the differences that having a new security system will make within a given timeframe. The linguistic (auditory) ambiguity 'by or buy this' is covertly suggesting that the prospect do just that. It is a powerful 'What lead' *pre-suppositional question*, as it presumes there will be some differences. Depending upon how the question is delivered, you might spot a *dispersed embedded command*, suggesting, 'buy this security system'.

Suggestion	Question
Want this	What do you really want this car for? A people carrier for family outings with the children or a workhorse to get from A to B delivering stock to your clients?

Analysis This powerful 'What lead' *pre-suppositional question* format embeds the command 'want this' or 'really want this' while appearing to enquire about how the client sees the principle use of the vehicle. The message to 'want this car' slips effortlessly into the subconscious mind of the listener, reinforcing desire as they consider how to answer the surface question.

Question format

The previous questions broadly follow this format:

What do you + want/need this + (product/service) to do for you/your company/this office

You will have noticed, throughout this section, the absence of the word 'why'. While high up on the persuasive scale for some, we would suggest minimising its use as a question opener, as it can be considered inquisitorial; it may induce a defensive response in some and, if repeated, will seem antagonistic. In most situations, a question beginning with 'why' can be reformed to begin with 'what'. Questions starting with 'How' and 'What' are inherently powerful and pre-suppositional.

brilliant tips

Correctly constructing your questions will give tremendous influence in either opening or narrowing the options available to your customer.

- Incorporate the vocabulary of *awareness* and *internal representation*, such as: notice, see, realise, aware, experience, discover, consider, contemplate, think about, what if, imagine, how about, if you could have. This will dramatically increase the effectiveness of your questioning technique.

- When you wish to evoke a 'yes' or 'no' response, ask questions beginning with: do, could, would or are.

- Formulate your questions in advance to ensure you receive the answers you want to hear.

- Do not over-complicate your questions, as those using familiar everyday words are accepted and answered more precisely.

- If you choose to embed commands into your questions, keep them short. The command should be a maximum of four words.

Now you are aware of how much more persuasive you will be when asking powerful questions, it is worrying to think about what will happen if you fail to do so. Isn't it? Imagine losing more business and paving the way for the competition. You have realised that getting close to your sales target can sometimes be a struggle. Haven't you?

Consider the reduction in your spending power if your bonus drops. What if job security became an issue? Let's face it, holding down a sales job in an increasingly competitive market is not easy, is it?

We are pleased to say that we do not want you to be concerned about any of this happening. Because it is our mission to ensure you never experience professional failure. You see, we are going to guide you smoothly and quickly through the process of acquiring the skills to quantum leap your questioning and persuasive abilities. Now, you can get really enthused about this, can't you?

brilliant recap

- Powerful questions:
  - are thought-provoking and invite your prospect(s) to reflect on ideas and issues and provide comprehensive answers;
  - can expand your customers, options and focus and direct their attention;
  - bring underlying assumptions to light and make assumptions indirectly;
  - can contain subliminal suggestions and hidden directives;
  - can stimulate curiosity and deepen interest;
  - can lead and guide your prospect towards your goal;
  - can move your conversations forward.

- To embed the commands 'want this' or 'need this', adapt this question structure to your business: What do you + want/need this + (product/service) to do for you/your company/this office?

- To direct your prospect to reaffirm what they have already stated and build the habit of saying 'yes', follow open questions with closed questions.

- Kipling questions are open questions and begin with the words: Why, What, Who, Where and When. To these we add: Which, What if and How.

- Closed questions are desirable when a yes/no answer is required and start with the words: Do, Could, Would, Is, and Are.

- Should your prospect answer 'yes/no because' in response to a closed question, observe their vocabulary following the word 'because', as it will reveal their motivational direction. You will be able to deepen rapport and lower resistance by continuing the conversation, reflecting their preferred vocabulary.

- Questions beginning with 'Where', 'How', 'What' and 'What if' are thought more compelling than questions beginning with 'Which', 'Who' and 'When'.

It is very likely you already use all of these questioning formats in your daily life, at work and home. Now, by consciously applying the appropriate kind of questioning, you can plant suggestions gain the information, response or outcome you seek even more efficiently.

CHAPTER 19

Future pacing or time-travel questions

Make your prospects crave for your products or services

'Sometimes questions are more important than answers.'

Nancy Willard

What is future pacing and how will you use it?

We have referred to this type of question rather light-heartedly in the chapter title as 'time travel' because it encourages your potential client to walk mentally into, and visualise, their future reality, void of the benefits offered by the services or products you are offering.

The acknowledged name for this language pattern, and the one we adopt for the remainder of this chapter, is future pacing. It works by encouraging your prospects to imagine vividly the negative impact and full consequences not embracing your offer will have on their lives. As with all, not least with this technique, rapport is the foundation of its success; without it, it will not succeed.

At this juncture, you might be wondering precisely how we accomplish the 'future pacing effect' and motivate others to think positively about our products and services or do what we want them to do. Curiously, you have already travelled to a distant future and experienced the journey towards the end of the last chapter. Do you recall reading the following passage? For clarity, the numbers refer to the specific language patterns and linguistic techniques we have used.

Now you are aware (1) of how much more persuasive you will be when asking powerful questions; it is worrying to think about (2) what will happen if you fail to do so (3). Isn't it? (4) Imagine (5) losing more business and paving the way for the competition (6). You have realised that (7) getting close to your sales target can sometimes be a struggle. Haven't you? (8)

Consider (9) the reduction in your spending power if your bonus drops. What if (10) job security became an issue? (11) Let's face it, holding down a sales job in an increasingly competitive market isn't easy, is it? (12)

We are pleased to say that we do not want you to be concerned about any of this happening. Because (13) it is our mission to ensure you never experience professional failure. You see, we are going to guide you smoothly and quickly through the process of acquiring the skills to quantum leap your questioning and persuasive abilities. Now, a person can get really enthused about this, can't you? (14)

Can you recollect the feelings it evoked and the thoughts that passed through your mind when you read this for the first time?

We deliberately exaggerated the technique by asking a lot of questions. Nevertheless their singular purpose was to encourage you to walk mentally into a dismal future and visualise yourself struggling to win business, having less money and being vulnerable to job security issues looming on the horizon. We included in those short paragraphs four *internal representations* and *tag questions*, two *awareness patterns* and three *powerful questions*, compelling you to envision and intensely dislike the potential future reality you had pictured so much that you would strive to ensure it did not happen by integrating *powerful persuasive questions* into your sales presentations.

Let us review what was said in those earlier paragraphs in more depth:

1	Awareness pattern	Aware
2	Internal representation	Think about
3	Pre-suppositional question	What will happen
4	Tag question	Isn't it?
5	Internal representation	Imagine
6	Negative suggestion	Losing more business and paving the way for competition
7	Awareness pattern	Realised
8	Tag question	Haven't you?
9	Internal representation	Consider
10	Internal representation	What if
11	Powerful question	Planting suggestion – job insecurity
12	Tag question	Is it?
13	Because logic	Because we want you to believe our mission
14	Tag question/pronoun shift	Can't you?

The structure of a future pacing question

The technique has two parts. In the first, we guide our prospects to visualise a future void of the benefits offered by our products and service and, in the second, we assure them it is our mission to ensure the future they have imagined will not happen.

Part one

Use the vocabulary of *internal representation* and *awareness* to pose powerful 'What', 'How' and 'What if' lead questions to ensure your prospect graphically pictures the adverse consequences, personal and/or corporate, that not progressing with your offer brings.

Vocabulary of internal representation	Vocabulary of awareness
Consider/considered	Notice
Think about	See
What if	Observe
Imagine/imagined	Realise
How about	Aware
If you could have	Experience
What would/will it be like if/when	Discover
Think through	Detect
Reflect on	

Part two

Part two is where all the difficulties are resolved as you advise your prospect that everything they have just imagined will not happen because it is your mission to guarantee it does not.

How to deliver future pacing questions

Both your manner and tone of voice are crucial to ensure the effectiveness of this technique. It is best to adopt a conversational style, as your questions should be articulated without particular emphasis and not marked out as you would, for example, at the beginning of a meeting, when broad questions are the norm because their purpose is to elicit information. Remember, you are asking rhetorical questions only to plant suggestions and ideas, a response is not necessarily required or expected. Unless it is evident that your prospect wishes to respond, move the conversation on gently once you have asked the question.

How to maximise the effectiveness of future pacing questions

Ask yourself, apart from the obvious advantages that owning your product will bring, what are the specific requirements your client desires? Do they need your product/service to:

● achieve a goal? (Towards-oriented) or

● prevent something from happening? (Away-oriented)

Identifying your prospect's motivational direction is especially valuable when composing future pacing questions for two reasons:

1   Rapport is strengthened, as you are talking the same language as your prospect.

2   You have identified how they go about achieving their objectives. Understanding this expertly enables you to describe graphically, in their preferred linguistic style, the consequences of failing to realise them.

brilliant tip

To identify a future pacing question, before your meeting, answer the following question on behalf of your prospect, 'Why is not buying your product or service not a good idea?' By answering this, you will identify the consequences and potential pain your prospect could experience by not buying what you are offering.

Future pacing a towards-oriented individual

Towards-oriented people are motivated by what they will gain and achieve. To future pace them, help them to imagine the consequences of failing to reach their objective, however they have defined it.

Future pacing an away-oriented individual

Away-oriented people are driven by a strong desire to prevent something from happening or they move away from a problem to achieve their goal. Help them to imagine the worst case scenario of that event taking place.

It is alarming, isn't it? Now you are aware how much more persuasive you will be when using future pacing questions and statements in your presentations, think about what will happen if you fail to do so.

Enjoy this technique; used wisely it will make a huge difference to your persuasive abilities.

brilliant recap

- One of the most powerful ways to persuade someone is to stimulate their imagination and enable them to visualise vividly the possible alarming outcomes that might occur, should they not accept your offer, before you reassure them that, whatever they have envisioned, will not happen, to their great relief!

- Future pacing is particularly effective when combined with the vocabulary of internal representation because this language stimulates the imagination of your subject.

- Use this technique discreetly in a conversational style for maximum effect.

- When asking future pacing questions do not necessarily expect an answer, because the purpose is to plant suggestions and 'What if' scenarios in your prospect's mind.

CHAPTER 20

Criteria questions

Establish what your prospects value most highly and make you product or service fit their needs

'Your beliefs become your thoughts. Your thoughts become your words. Your words become your actions. Your actions become your habits. Your habits become your values and your values become your destiny.'

Mahatma Gandhi

C riteria refers to the values important to us that determine how we make decisions. Understanding the basis upon which others make decisions enables us to formulate irresistibly persuasive sales presentations. Have you ever considered what motivates your decision-making process? How much more effective would you be if you understood the driving force behind the choices your prospects make when considering to buy your products or retain your services?

The criteria or core values to which we refer whenever making decisions are deeply seated within us all. Criteria questioning allows us to bring our prospects' values to the surface and attach them to the particular benefits and advantages offered by our products or services. By doing this, we are helping our potential customers to verbalise and understand their reasons for taking certain actions and, as it is *their* reasoning, they will recognise the criteria and be much more likely to follow through and engage your services or purchase your products.

Stage one

How to discover your prospect's core values or criteria – method one

The process of identifying your prospect's *core values* or *criteria* is much simpler than you may, at first, think and involves asking a couple of powerful questions. It is how and when you ask these questions that requires forethought and planning.

In stage one, the question you have to ask your prospect is, 'What's important to you about . . . ?' When we ask this question, we are eliciting information about what our prospect needs to happen or to have before they can consider working with or buying from you. This type of question is also called a *value* or *needs elicitation question*.

Here are a few examples.

---

brilliant examples

- What's important to you about working with a company/agency like (agency/company name)?
- What's important to you about the next house you want to buy?
- What's important to you about your next car?
- What's important to you about correctly investing your savings?
- What's important to you about going to the gym?
- What's important to you about the next hardware upgrade?

Once your prospect answers this style of question, you have the core criteria against which decisions are made. Make a mental note or write down the specific words they use; this is of particular significance because, later, you will repeat the identical phrase back to them.

If you are presenting to a multi-functional team, direct your value elicitation questions to the most influential members of the group. Each function, sales, engineering and finance, will have specific areas of critical importance that will impact in different ways on their decisions to proceed.

How to discover your prospect's core values or criteria – method two

Once you have asked the 'What's important to you about X?' question, in some circumstances, your prospect's opening response, while important and in itself revealing, may not be their core criteria. Occasionally, at this first stage of questioning, the initial answer might be a sweeping generalisation. Should you sense this is the case, steer your prospect towards volunteering their deeper core values, by repeating the questioning process.

---

brilliant example

Persuader	Before we go further, I wonder if I can ask, what's important about working with a consultancy like Stephen St James & Associates?
Prospect	The main *advantage* is your firm has a track record in our industry.
Persuader	Yes, having market intelligence is crucial. What's particularly important about this to your company?
Prospect	Your expertise *enables* us to specifically target people from our sector so they can start running from day one.
Persuader	Seems like there is some urgency. Every company has slightly different ways of going about things – what's so important he has to start running from day one?
Prospect	These are troubled times. The incumbent couldn't be leaving at a worse time; there's a lot of pressure on HR to *secure* a high calibre candidate and move the business forwards.

The value elicitation process above initially yielded the broadest response, 'track record', and further questioning produced the response, 'secure high calibre people and move the business forwards'. Having posed three *elicitation questions*, it is appropriate to accept this answer. Imagine taking this questioning process a step further: ultimately, if ever you have an opportunity to do this, financial freedom and personal security surface quite frequently.

Relating personal security and financial freedom to the advantages of your product/service is very powerful.

Stage two

Combining core values to benefits

Now, using your prospect's vocabulary, link the advantages and benefits of your product/service to their core values. These are the answers you received to your elicitation questions. Using their language like this is imperative because it makes your proposition irresistible; you are giving them, in their words, exactly what they have already indicated they want.

---

brilliant example

Returning to our example, the persuader, at some point during the meeting, might say:

Persuader   That's right. The main advantage we have compared
                         to other recruiters is not only our current understand-
                         ing of the market but also we know the whereabouts
                         of high calibre candidates. Our insight enables us
                         to take the pressure off you and ensure the human
                         resources department performs well and secures the
                         highest calibre candidate to help move the business
                         forwards.

Response analysis   The prospect's core criteria, that of reducing the pres-
                         sure and stress in the human resources department,
                         securing candidates and moving the business
                         forwards, are intermingled with the inherent advan-
                         tages provided by the consultancy they are about to
                         appoint.

Motivational direction

There is something quite subtle you have learnt, once you have elicited the final value response. You have identified the motivational direction of your prospect. In our example, the last response was:

> *Prospect*   These are troubled times. Pete couldn't be leaving at a worse time; there's a lot of pressure on HR to secure a high calibre candidate and move the business forwards.

In the earlier dialogue the prospect used the words 'enables', 'advantage' and 'secure', which reveal a towards-linguistic preference. The persuader cleverly introduces the same vocabulary into his/her presentation.

The last words from the persuader were:

> *Persuader*   That's right. The main *advantage* we have compared to other recruiters is not only our current understanding of the market but also we know the whereabouts of *high calibre candidates*. Our insight *enables* us to take the pressure off you and ensure the *HR department performs* well and *secures* the *highest calibre candidate* to help *move the business forwards*.

This response subtly reflects both the *motivational direction* and *core criteria* of the prospect and will appeal to client, as the value of the external consultant is reinforced in their linguistic style.

Weasel phrases or openers

Asking questions repeatedly beginning with 'what' and 'when' can, at times, appear inquisitorial, so, to bypass the adverse effects posing such questions can occasionally have on others, we chose to soften their delivery by using *weasel* or *opening phrases*. Below, we have reproduced the persuader's questions. Can you spot the weasel phrases?

Persuader   Before we go further, I wonder if I can ask, what's important about working with a consultancy like Stephen St James & Associates?

Persuader   Yes, having that market intelligence is crucial. What's particularly important about this to your company?

Persuader   Seems like there is some urgency. Every company has slightly different ways of going about things – what's so important he has to start running from day one?

Some opening phrases are art forms in themselves; essentially, when you know you are about to ask repeated questions beginning with the words 'what' or 'when', plan to soften their delivery. The more you think about doing this, the more it will become second nature.

The weasel or opening phrases above are:

● Before we go further, I wonder if I can ask . . .

● Yes, having that market intelligence is crucial.

● Every company has slightly different ways of going about things.

Just about anything said before the word 'what' can be considered a *weasel phrase*.

Alternative questioning method

Many favour progressively dispersing criteria questions within the conversation, preferring not to ask them one after another, as in the above example. When the value elicitation process is interspersed throughout the discussion, the persuader makes a mental note of the core values expressed and picks their moment to feed them back to their prospect.

brilliant recap

- When your prospect repeats the same answer, you have attained the highest core value you can achieve within the context of that conversation.

- Observe the speed of the responses you receive. Often, the quickest response reveals the highest core value. Should your prospect ponder over their answers, the most significant value has yet to be expressed.

- Ask a maximum of three or four elicitation questions.

- Ensure you have developed a sufficient level of rapport in advance of attempting this questioning technique.

- Ideally, raise the 'What's important to you?' question during a conversation where many questions are being asked back and forth; this seemingly buries the question and its importance will appear diminished as your potential prospect responds in a relaxed manner.

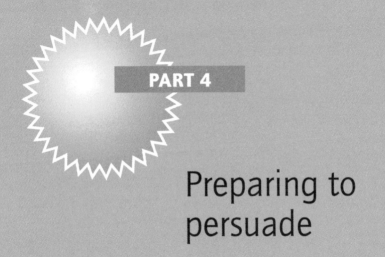

PART 4

Preparing to persuade

CHAPTER 21

Questions to ask yourself

Prepare yourself for every outcome and consequence

'"Would you tell me, please, which way I ought to go from here?"

"That depends a good deal on where you want to get to," said the Cat.

"I don't much care where," said Alice.

"Then it doesn't matter which way you go," said the Cat.

"So long as I get somewhere," Alice added as an explanation.

"Oh, you're sure to do that," said the Cat, "if you only walk long enough."'

Lewis Carroll, *Alice in Wonderland*

How often, when in a client meeting, have you found yourself preoccupied and drifting off, allowing others to take the lead while you are supposed to be paying attention? Have you ever felt disconnected from your prospect and lost in your thoughts?

Up to now, we have targeted our attention towards our prospective customers and the questions we ask them to acquire information and, most significantly, plant suggestions. While always appreciating the importance of asking powerful questions of others, preparation and focus are fundamental to your success. To facilitate higher degrees of both, in this chapter, we are going to direct our attention towards two sets of questions that we ask ourselves.

What is important about asking ourselves questions?

In a nutshell, focus and knowledge. With knowledge comes understanding, as we acquaint ourselves with our potential clients' requirements and their circumstances. With intense focus, you will acquire heightened awareness of your prospect's needs, together with a deeper appreciation of exactly how your offering matches them.

The first set of questions are Cartesian and are named after the seventeenth-century French philosopher René Descartes.

Descartes is considered by many as the founding father of modern philosophy. In our view, some fundamental principles of persuasion are rooted in his philosophical teachings. We are going to ask ourselves four Cartesian questions, formed initially for solving problems with logic. These questions force us to think outside of the box and, by thinking laterally like this, we intensify our awareness of our prospect's situation in ways we, otherwise, might have missed.

To reflect the necessities of the twenty-first century and our particular requirements, we have updated the questions. Their structure, however, remains the same.

Cartesian questions

In preparation for every presentation, answer these questions comprehensively. Your answers will be different for every prospect.

1 *Why is buying your product/service a good idea?*

   List the main advantages, other than the obvious ones, that your prospect will enjoy about your product/service. List as many as you can, as you never know which one(s) will strike a chord with your customer.

2 *Why is not buying your product/service a good idea?*

   These are the objections your potential customers and competition will raise. Identify your own and reframe them, accentuating the positive using this sentence structure:

   The issue isn't X, the issue is Y + and that means Z and/or ask a question

   ● X is the reason your prospect may not buy your product/ service.

   ● Y is a positive aspect of your product/service that you wish to bring to the attention of your prospect.

   ● Z is anything you want to be related to Y that brings the conversation more closely towards your outcome.

⏵ brilliant example

Prospect	I hear your customer support is pretty poor. I am sorry we could not invest in such a highly priced product with poor after-sales support.
Persuader	*The issue isn't* about what you might have heard about our after-sales support services. *The issue is* our products have the highest reputation for quality in the market and, unlike others, are designed specifically for your requirements. *And that means* because so much attention is given at the start, to 'design in' your requirements, support costs are lower. What's important to you about having us design your product specifically for your needs?
Response analysis	In the first part of the redefine, the word 'heard' sneakily places the objection in the past. We did not say, 'what you might *hear* in the market'. It is always advantageous to linguistically place objections in the past, as it subliminally implies they are historical.
	The second part of the redefine emphasises positive aspects of the product. We continue by saying, 'and that means' and it can mean anything we want! We then say 'because' because most people more readily accept whatever follows it as true. Finally, we ask a compelling 'what lead', pre-suppositional question to redirect the conversation towards the most critical areas.

3 *Why is buying your product or service not a good idea?*

Here you are looking for the minor negative aspects of your service. Most sales professionals overlook this concept. Psychological research validates the power of this counter-intuitive approach; when you argue against your point of view/self-interest, you will appear unbiased. Note: list only *minor* negative aspects!

4   *Why is not buying your product or service not a good idea?*

This question identifies the consequences and pain that your prospect will experience by not buying what you are offering.

Cartesian questions are inclined to scramble your brain a little, and that is the point! They compel you to think outside of the box and prepare you for virtually any conversational manoeuvre when face to face with a potential customer.

The next set of questions are somewhat easier, and we would suggest completing them in detail before every meeting with a new prospect.

Pre-contact questions

- At the end of my sales meeting, how would I like to feel?

- How, specifically, would I like my potential client to feel?

- What is my personal objective?

- What is significant to me about this sales presentation?

- How much time have I assigned for this meeting?

- Have I and my potential customer allocated sufficient time for this encounter?

- How will my client be better off when they purchase my product or service?

- What are the important dates, timeframes and costs?

- Do I have all the information I need? Is anything missing?

- What is the worst thing that could take place?

- Can I make this presentation on my own? What benefit is gained involving others?

- What questions should I ask to evoke interest? (Make a list of pre-suppositional questions.)

- What current challenges does my potential client have and how can my product/service resolve them?

- What questions will I be asked? (List them and your response.)

- What will my customer find most and least appealing about my product/service/company/me?

- What, specifically, interests my prospect about my product/service today?

- What reasons might influence why my potential customer may not be interested in my product/service today? (Make a list.)

Without a doubt, there is a little crossover between the Cartesian and the pre-contact questions that is only to your advantage. By answering these questions, you will be more focused towards your prospect and your goals and be fully prepared to ask relevant pre-suppositional questions and, significantly, you will be fully equipped to respond to any questions or objections directed at you.

The missing question

There is one question we have not included in the above list because it is applicable only for those who experience confidence or belief issues relating to the product/service they are selling. It is entirely possible to learn techniques to persuade but, if you are doubtful about the veracity of your product or service, it will be almost impossible to sell consistently. You see, your doubts are visible and read by others in your body language; you cannot help it. Your non-verbal communication is opposed to what you are expressing verbally and your prospects will pick this up on a subliminal level. Being very honest with yourself, ask:

- What is preventing me from being certain the product/service I am promoting is of value to my prospect?

Ponder this question on your own, then ask a more successful colleague what is important to them about what they are selling, you noticed it's a criteria question, didn't you? You may not wish to share your personal doubts, but this is a good starting point.

brilliant tip

To boost your confidence, answer the questions in this chapter repeatedly for every business development and sales opportunity. By doing so, you will be more client-centred and focused on the mission at hand. You will, subliminally, exude confidence, which your prospect will pick up and absorb.

brilliant recap

- Always have an outcome in mind. It can be an invitation to meet again, to make an appointment to meet another company representative or to make a sale.
- Asking questions of ourselves is as important as directing them towards our prospects.
- List the standard objections to your product or service and reframe them.
- The more scenarios we have in our mind about possible outcomes, the more prepared we are when they happen.
- List all the reasons why your potential client would and would not want your product or service.
- List and reframe all possible objections others might harbour towards your products and services. Remember, this could be what the competition is saying about you!

CHAPTER 22

Building natural confidence

Develop the confidence to persuade

'Building confidence is like building an empire, nobody notices the ground work, but the output commands attention on its own.'

Unknown

Let's face it; if you want to be persuasive, you must be confident. In this chapter, we reveal how you can heighten your level of confidence across all aspects of your life. Have you ever dreamt so vividly you doubted it was a dream? A favourite of many, and I use the word favourite guardedly, is, when sleeping, we suddenly so realistically fall down a flight stairs, off a cliff or trip over something and wake with a jolt, consciously experiencing real shock.

I suspect everyone has, and will continue to have, these dream state experiences. The technique you are about to learn harnesses the benefits of the subconscious mind's inability to differentiate between a dream and reality.

An effective way of enhancing a particular behaviour, or creating a new one, is to vividly visualise ourselves as if you already possess the improved behaviour we seek. The more powerfully we imagine yourselves the way you want to be, the more these images and associated emotions become embedded into your subconscious mind and become our reality.

Once you become an expert in the technique you are about to discover you can apply it to many different aspects of your life that you wish to enhance. Essentially, we imagine what we will look and feel like with the behaviour we seek, then physically link an emotion to the improved behaviour. By using our imagination, we can 'test run' and experience the behaviour we want because:

● We can acquire new behaviours by forming powerful images of ourselves from different perspectives. When you start to see yourself more favourably and embed those images into your subconscious, with practice and repetition, the dream or vision becomes your reality.

● The more comprehensively we imagine ourselves with the behaviour we seek, the greater the likelihood of it becoming our reality.

● Who you are today is the accumulation of your experience. Visualise now whom you want to become tomorrow.

● You already possess the mental resources required to achieve your goal; your success is determined by your ability to tap into them.

State your goal

If this is your first attempt at something like this, I ask that you have faith and an open mind; this technique is very effective and, with patience and regular practice, will produce the results you seek. The key is to state your goal unambiguously from the outset, today we will focus on building confidence.

Basic steps

1 Ask yourself, if I was already highly confident, what would I look like?

2 Visualise yourself as if you were already highly confident.

3 Exaggerate the images of yourself and the emotions you feel and make a physical link between the two.

4 Mentally jump into your alter ego and become absorbed in the images and emotions you have created.

In the embellished version of the above, which follows, we suggest you move your eyes in specific directions to coincide with particular requests:

● Move your eyes down to your left when you *ask* yourself something.

● Move your eyes up to your left or right when you *see* yourself doing something.

Without conscious thought, most people's eyes move in these directions, as they have either an internal dialogue with themselves or imagine something. The experience and effectiveness of this technique is heightened by consciously accompanying the requests with hitherto unconscious eye movements.

1   Close your eyes and imagine yourself in your local cinema. In front of you is an imaginary screen. *With your eyes down to your left*, ask yourself, if I was already more confident, what would I look like?

2   *With your eyes up to your left or right*, see yourself sitting in the cinema, looking up at a super confident version of yourself displayed on the screen.

brilliant tips

If you need help visualising the most confident you, experiment with some of the scenarios below. Jump to step 3 if you are a natural visualiser.

● *With your eyes down and to your left*, ask yourself if there is a small part of being more confident you can visualise. *With your eyes up and to your right*, see yourself on the film screen performing that tiny part of your overall goal. You might see yourself standing alone at a dinner party, but feeling supremely at ease.

● *With your eyes up and to your right*, see others being drawn to you as you exude confidence.

▶

● *With your eyes down and to your left*, ask yourself when was the last time you felt a little confident, then, *with your eyes up and to your right*, see yourself in that same situation again. This time, positively exaggerate the image of yourself and the circumstances. Change the outcome, intensify how you felt and the degree of confidence you felt.

● Your body language subconsciously indicates your level of confidence. In your film, see yourself with powerful body language and increased levels of eye contact with others.

● Do you know someone who possesses the confidence you crave? *With your eyes down and to your left*, ask yourself, 'Who is the most confident person I know?' Then, *with your eyes up and to your right*, see them in whatever situation, exhibiting the confidence you want, then immediately see yourself as them doing exactly as they are doing. Deeply tune in to how it must feel to be them at that moment.

3　Still *with your eyes up to your left or right*, as you see yourself watching the screen, embellish the images of your super confident self, make them bigger and bolder, better quality, crisper and brighter and closer. *With your eyes and head down and to your right*, think about how being ultra-confident feels, hold on to and intensify that feeling as you see yourself slowly standing up and walking towards the screen.

4　*With your eyes and head down and to your right*, intensify the feelings even more. Now, slowly rise from your seat and see yourself standing directly in front of the film screen, looking at a larger than life super confident film of yourself. Your emotions are heightened. As you experience being the person you are watching, begin imagining how it feels to be the ultra-confident you. Notice how you feel the tremendous power of your confidence throughout your body; start to experience it in your imagination.

As your emotions peak and your feeling of confidence is strongest, squeeze the thumbs and forefingers of both hands together and forever associate the sense of being superbly confident with that physical action. Now, mentally jump into the screen and into the super-sized confident you that you have created and experience what it is like to be super confident.

How to use this technique
Every time you want to revisit these positive, successful experiences of being more confident, squeeze your thumb and forefinger and relive the images and emotions you experienced in this process. Empower yourself and do this before your next sales presentation.

brilliant tips

- At first, it might be advisable to ask someone to read out loud the various steps until you are able to complete the exercise on your own.
- Take your time learning this technique. You will find it well worth the effort. Practise every day, one step at a time, until you can link all the steps together effortlessly.
- Refer to the basic explanation, then to the embellished version to increase your familiarity with the process.

brilliant recap

- When you first attempt this technique, omit the directions relating to your eye movements; you may find your eyes move naturally to these points without conscious thought.

▶

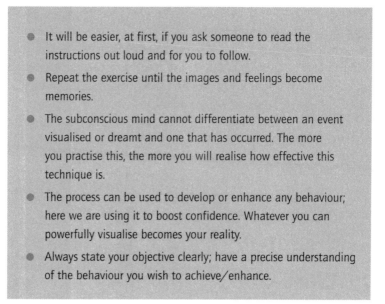

- It will be easier, at first, if you ask someone to read the instructions out loud and for you to follow.
- Repeat the exercise until the images and feelings become memories.
- The subconscious mind cannot differentiate between an event visualised or dreamt and one that has occurred. The more you practise this, the more you will realise how effective this technique is.
- The process can be used to develop or enhance any behaviour; here we are using it to boost confidence. Whatever you can powerfully visualise becomes your reality.
- Always state your objective clearly; have a precise understanding of the behaviour you wish to achieve/enhance.

CHAPTER 23

How to practise

'The difference between ordinary and extraordinary is practice.'

Vladimir Horowitz

W hen you are not practising the techniques in *Brilliant Persuasion*, remember that someone somewhere else is, and it might be your competition!

Congratulate yourself for progressing to this point in your studies about persuasion. To fully grasp the techniques and increase your familiarity with their use, you must do more than merely read this book. To move forwards towards fluency with your new persuasive vocabulary and style of communication, it is essential to allocate time to daily practice and fine-tune your developing skills.

Practice stage one

Rapport confidence and focus

First, I would like you to place all but three of the techniques you have learnt to a quiet corner of your mind and leave them there while concentrating on the following patterns only for the next week, or until you feel comfortable to progress further.

● *Rapport*

Without rapport, persuasion is impossible, so look for every possible opportunity to use the *instant rapport technique*, outlined in Chapter 5, and carefully monitor the reactions you receive.

● *Pre-contact and Cartesian questions*

For every business meeting during the next week, concentrate intensely on preparation by answering, in detail, the pre-contact questions and Cartesian questions in Chapter 21. Then, in the actual client/prospect meeting, do not try to use any language patterns, instead take notice of how you are feeling being super prepared.

● *Confidence*

At every opportunity, revisit Chapter 22 about building natural confidence and follow the step-by-step guide, until you have thoroughly mastered visualising yourself being highly confident and you can bring to the surface the positive emotions associated with the images you have created.

brilliant tip

Before attempting any language pattern with a real client or prospect, concentrate on re-reading Chapters 5, 21 and 22 until you have truly mastered: developing rapport, pre-contact preparation and building confidence. If this is all you do for the next week, it will be time well spent because we want you to learn these techniques before using any other patterns.

During the time you spend developing rapport, start intently listening to colleagues, family members and friends using language patterns without awareness, in everyday conversations. Carefully monitor corporate advertising and listen to talk shows on the TV and radio. Remember, most people are unaware they use language patterns every day.

Practice stage two

Pick your favourite pattern

Once you have spent time revisiting Chapters 5, 21 and 22, and have experienced the benefits the techniques discussed can bring, it is time to progress to the next practice stage and to start introducing your favourite patterns into everyday conversations at home with family and friends and at work with your colleagues.

Review the patterns

Choose a couple of your favourite patterns and rehearse them with imaginary prospects. Create scenarios, formulate objections and prepare your responses. Start saying the patterns out loud, often.

Business meetings

By now, you have, almost certainly, read this book more than once. You will have spent time enhancing your ability to develop rapport and personal focus. You will have decided upon some favourite patterns and experimented using them with family and friends. Now, it is time to use a pattern at your next business meeting.

It is a good idea when using language patterns for the first time in a business setting that the meeting is not the most important one in your calendar, and you have chosen a few favourite patterns.

For example, during the meeting, you may say only 'You, like me . . . etc.' This is your first *embedded command*. Alternatively, you may ask a 'What lead' *pre-suppositional question* – this is your first powerful question. The point is, while you may be articulating phrases and sentences that you would normally say, crucially, now you aware they are language patterns and you will proactively choose to use them.

Repetition

As soon as you deliver a pattern, observe the response and, as your confidence builds, add more. It is important to progress slowly by gradually adding patterns as your confidence increases and, soon, you will see how effortlessly they slip through the net, unnoticed.

Results take time, so be patient. If a pattern does not come out right first time, just try again; you have nothing to lose and everything to gain.

brilliant recap

- Reading about persuasion alone will not boost your powers of persuasion and influence. Regular practice is essential to build your confidence and familiarise yourself with the word combinations revealed in these chapters.

- To ensure that the techniques we have described work for you, learn to develop resonant rapport. If this challenges you, visualise what you would look like, having developed rapport, and follow the same steps for developing natural confidence in Chapter 22.

- Acquire a thorough understanding of what your prospect wants to gain from meeting you and, crucially, what you need from a commercial and a personal perspective.

- With your newly found linguistic insight, acutely listen to others in conversation and notice how often, without awareness, they use the language patterns.

- Pick a few language patterns with which you are instantly comfortable and use them with family and friends in meetings, where there is no stress.

- Be patient and repeat the techniques you are acquiring as often as you can; even talk to yourself, if no one is around, until they flow naturally into your everyday conversations.

Appendix
The most persuasive words

A

Abolish
Absolutely
Accelerate
Achieve
Act
Adopt
Advice
Align
Amazing
Announcing
Anticipate
Anticipation
Appeal
Apply
Appreciative
Approve
Assess
Attention
Attract
Authentic
Avoid
Aware

B

Bargain
Beautiful
Because
Believe
Benefit
Best
Big
Blown out
Boost

Brand name
Break
Bridge
Bright
Budget
Build
Burn
Buy

C

Call
Capture
Care
Challenge
Change
Choose
Clarify
Clearance
Compare
Complete
Comprehend
Confidential
Confront
Connect
Conquer
Consider
Convenient
Convert
Create
Cross

D

Decide
Define

Defuse
Delicious
Deliver
Dependable
Deploy
Deserve
Design
Develop
Development
Diagnose
Direct
Discover
Drastically
Drive

E

Easy
Eliminate
Endorse
Ensure
Establish
Evaluate
Excellent
Exciting
Exclusive
Experience
Expert
Exploit
Explore
Extravaganza

F

Fabulous
Fact
Family
Famous
Fantastic
Fascinating
Fast
Feel
Filter
Finalise
Find
Focus

Foresee
Fortune
Free
Fresh
Full

G

Gain
Game
Gather
Generate
Genuine
Get
Gigantic
Give
Goal
Grasp
Great
Guarantee

H

Have
Health
Hello
Help
Helpful
Honest
Hurry

I

Identity
Ignite
Illuminate
Imagine
Implement
Important
Improve
Increase
Incredible
Information
Innovate
Inspire
Intensify

Interesting
Invited

K

Keep
Knowledge

L

Largest
Latest
Lead
Learn
Leverage
Lifetime
Limited
Look
Love
Low

M

Magic
Manage
Master
Maximise
Measure
Miracle
Mobilise
Modern
Money
More
Most
Motivate

N

Need
New
News
Notice
Now

O

Offer
Official
Open
Opportunity

Outstanding
Overcome

P

Penetrate
Personalised
Persuade
Plan
Please
Popular
Position
Powerful
Practical
Prepare
Present
Prevent
Price
Professional
Profit
Profitable
Protect
Proud
Proven

Q

Qualified
Quality
Quick

R

Raise
Rare
Ready
Real
Realise
Reassurance
Recommended
Reconsider
Redeemable
Reduce
Referred
Refresh
Refundable
Relax

Reliable
Remarkable
Replace
Reputation
Resist
Respond
Responsible
Results
Retain
Revolutionary
Reward
Rich
Right
Rush

S

Safety
Satisfaction
Save
Scan
Secret
Secure
Security
See
Segment
Selected
Selection
Self-confident
Sensational
Service
Shatter
Shave off
Sidestep
Simple
Simplify
Smart
Smile
Smoothly
Solve
Special
Start
Startling
Stimulate
Stop

Stretch
Strong
Sturdy
Succeed
Successful
Suddenly
Superior
Supplement
Support
Suppose
Surprise

T

Take
Team
Terrific
Tested
Thank you
Time
Today
Train
Transfer
Transform
Tremendous
Trust
Try

U

Ultimate
Unconditional
Understand
Unique
Unleash
Unlimited
Use
Useful

V

Valuable
Vast

W

Want
Wanted

Warranty

Welcome

Well

Whittle down

Win

Wind

Wise

Wonderful

Y

Yes

You

Youthful

Further reading

Here are just some of the books I have reviewed and, more accurately, re-read while preparing *Brilliant Persuasion*. I have purchased all these books and suggest they will be valuable additions to your library and future studies.

Bowden, M. (2010) *Winning Body Language: Control the Conversation, Command Attention, and Convey the Right Message Without Saying a Word,* McGraw-Hill

Caldini, R. (2009) *Influence: The Psychology of Persuasion,* HarperCollins

Corah, M. (2012) *The Persuader: How To Use Emotional Persuasion to Win More Business,* Bookshaker

Hogan, K. and Speakman, J. (2006) *Covert Persuasion: Pyschological Tactics and Tricks to Win the Game,* John Wiley & Sons

Lakhani, D. (2005) *Persuasion: The Art of Getting What You Want,* John Wiley & Sons

Lakin, D. (2012) *The Unfair Advantage: Sell with NLP!,* Lakin Associates

Mesmer, F. (2011) *Unfair Secrets of Hypnotic Selling With NLP,* CreateSpace Independent Publishing Platform

Vitale, J. (2007) *Buying Trances: A New Pyschology of Sales and Marketing*, John Wiley & Sons

Webb, K. (2015) *The Language Pattern Bible: Indirect Hypnotherapy Patterns of Influence*, Best Buddy Books

Index